Teach-Practice-Apply:
The TPA Instruction Model, 7–12

The Authors

Judy Reinhartz is Associate Professor and Assistant Director of the Center for Professional Teacher Education at the University of Texas at Arlington. She is the coauthor of *Teach-Practice-Apply: The TPA Instruction Model, K-8* and of *Improving Middle School Instruction: A Research-Based Self-Assessment System*, and the editor of *Perspectives on Effective Teaching and the Cooperative Classroom*, published by NEA. She also developed the NEA In-Service Training Program *Effective Teaching and the Cooperative Classroom*.

Dennis Reinhartz is Associate Professor of History and Russian at the University of Texas at Arlington.

Teach-Practice-Apply:
The TPA Instruction Model, 7–12

by Judy Reinhartz
   Dennis Reinhartz

nea PROFESIONAL LIBRARY
National Education Association
Washington, D.C.

To our first teachers, our fathers,
Louis Gervasi and Paul Reinhartz.

—Judy Reinhartz
Dennis Reinhartz

Printing History
First Printing: April 1988

Note

The opinions expressed in this publication should not be construed as representing the policy or position of the National Education Association. Materials published by the NEA Professional Library are intended to be discussion documents for educators who are concerned with specialized interests of the profession.

Library of Congress Cataloging-in-Publication Data

Reinhartz, Judy.
    Teach-practice-apply: the TPA instruction model, 7–12 / by Judy Reinhartz, Dennis Reinhartz.
        p. cm.—(Developments in classroom instruction)
    Bibliography: p.
    ISBN 0–8106–1834–6
    1. Instructional systems—United States.   2. High school teaching—United States.   3. Concept learning.   4. Activity programs in education.   I. Reinhartz, Dennis.   II. Title.   III. Series.
LB1028.35.R44 1988
371.3–dc19   88–1576
                                                                            CIP

® 14

CONTENTS

PREFACE

In the early eighties educators were inundated with reports from a variety of sources, dealing with schooling, the quality of teaching, and classroom life. The mounting criticism resulting from these findings led to a general public dissatisfaction with the quality of elementary, secondary—and more recently—higher education. Not surprisingly, then, as Goodlad (46)* visited schools across the United States, he found teachers teaching the way they were taught, instructional sameness in both elementary and secondary schools. It is this problem of blandness, or one way of teaching, that this book attempts to address.

We assume that most secondary teachers know "what" to teach and "want" to teach it. We also assume that they will teach such essentials as outlining and study skills. But while they know their subjects, they often need more diversity in their approach to teaching. Using a variety of teaching strategies enables secondary teachers to better communicate their subject matter to their students, as well as to help their students develop problem-solving strategies in a variety of contexts. The goal of this text is to offer secondary teachers an alternative teaching model to improve their classroom delivery. This model includes a number of strategies and is supported by practical examples.

The proposed alternative instruction model is based on the teach-practice-apply (TPA) paradigm (84). This paradigm provides a structure for facilitating change, while ensuring the enhancement of instructional effectiveness. After describing several characteristics of effective instruction based on current research, we provide suggestions that secondary teachers can use in their classrooms.

Subsequent chapters elucidate the steps inherent in the use of each strategy, provide practice followup activities for teachers in the "Applying Your Knowledge" sections, and list assessment criteria for self-evaluation. Although the teaching strategies differ

---

*Numbers in parentheses appearing in the text refer to the Bibliography beginning on page 96.

from one another, the TPA model provides a unifying structure that allows teachers to acquire and implement them. Practical examples also are provided in various subject areas—social studies, science, mathematics, English, foreign languages, and the arts—to illustrate the implementation of each strategy.

We should also mention that, in contrast with the first five chapters, which are more conceptually based, Chapters 6 through 8 provide more concrete, hands-on activities because of the practical nature of the strategies involved.

We believe that secondary teachers can develop a mindset for change. By diversifying their instructional repertoire, they can better meet the complex needs of their adolescent students. The process of change often is difficult, dislocating, and time-consuming. Any efforts to achieve it must therefore be closely monitored by the teachers themselves as they engage in the process. We believe that this text provides a structural model to facilitate change—to help teachers learn and use alternative strategies and to gauge their own professional progress. We also hope that they will be encouraged to go beyond the strategies presented in the text and to use the TPA model as a basis for further creative endeavors in their classrooms. Such creativity can only stimulate their students—it is catching!

Chapter 1
A VIEW OF MASTERY SECONDARY INSTRUCTION

THE STATE OF THE ART

Although the teaching-learning process is extremely complex, critics consistently seek to simplify it. While trying to comprehend and improve it, these critics recommend numerous models, proposals, and studies concerning effective teaching. Despite all the current data, however, there are those who say with authority that "no one really knows what makes a good teacher." While there may be common attributes to effective teaching, no *one* factor has been discerned as definitive (75). For the critics, the research on effective instruction is described as "a cup half empty rather than half full" (14). For the optimists, the research of the past twenty years has identified common attributes associated with effective teaching (91).

The effective use of research on good teaching is a significant first step beyond knowledge alone. Current studies indicate a strong linkage between specific instructional attributes and desired student outcomes (49). Many critics are content with merely evaluating teachers. Medley (73), on the other hand, believes that evaluation also should include measuring student achievement. What, then, do effective teachers do differently from ineffective ones, and how do effective teachers increase student achievement?

Effective teachers have been shown to have specific managerial, instructional, and organizational attributes that set them apart from their more ineffective counterparts (85). These attributes are derived from comprehensive reviews of the literature and can be applied in classrooms (69, 91, 92, 121). Theoretical explanations gleaned from research studies when used by concerned teachers can lead to effective teaching (82). They can help teachers increase their "capacity to reach more students and to create a rich and more diverse environment for them" (61).

Teachers spend very little time analyzing their own teaching behavior. There are numerous reasons for this lack of self-analysis

9

and reflection. According to Jackson (56), Duffy and McIntryre (29), and Good and Brophy (42), teachers do not have the time or the training for such activities; they rely heavily on published materials as their guide. Hence, secondary teachers need to learn to analyze what they do and why they do it against a tapestry of what is known about effective teaching behaviors. Before discussing individual teaching attributes, however, a word of caution should be sounded.

Describing effective teaching is a difficult task because the research findings tend to be situation specific. Griffin (49) warns against overgeneralizing about the results of effective teaching research; often the findings apply to a specific grade level with a given student population. In addition, much of the research on teaching is correlational. That is, there is a high inference that positive student outcomes will result, but there are no guarantees—only a strong likelihood that the results can be duplicated. Despite such precautions, practitioners also need to be aware of the art as well as the science of teaching (30, 95).

The research findings reported here are from representative studies. They include a blend of qualitative and quantitative dimensions that may prove helpful to secondary teachers. These findings can only be beneficial, however, if teachers transfer them into their classrooms. The following section discusses attributes of effective teaching that are common and applicable to several curriculum areas. In addition, major research studies are cited to support these common attributes of good teachers and good teaching.

THE TECHNICAL CORE

One of the more noteworthy studies on content and sequencing for instruction, conducted by Fitzpatrick (36), involved ninth grade algebra and foreign language students and teachers. In this study, the control teachers behaved differently from those in the treatment group. The treatment teachers were given several suggestions about what was to be taught as well as a study manual. In addition, they held meetings to discuss the manual. The teachers in the control group were given only a manual; as a result, their teaching included less interaction with their students.

10

All teachers were observed in the same class for a total of five times. From the results Fitzpatrick found that the treatment teachers established expectations, attended to misbehaviors more frequently, kept students' attention, provided immediate evaluation and feedback, and maintained a warm and supportive environment (91). The results in each of these categories were lower for teachers in the control group.

One could generalize beyond the mathematics and foreign language in the preceding example by emphasizing that teachers need to be very familiar with the instructional sequence as well as with the skills and concepts inherent in the subject. The recommendations derived from the Fitzpatrick study are essential for teaching regardless of subject area. Structuring and sequencing any learning experience helps students better understand the content being presented. Familiarity with content can be obtained by reading a manual, but, more importantly, it is achieved by discussing the content with other teachers and a facilitator. Dialoguing with colleagues—in a sense, coaching each other in the use of the manual—assists teachers in going beyond the printed page. In addition, helping teachers by offering specific suggestions about teaching principles related to the content area increases their instructional effectiveness.

Quality of schooling includes not only time on task, but also time spent on such teaching practices as encouragement, corrective feedback, small group discussions, individualization, and student involvement (41). The use of classroom time, then, is another important attribute of teaching effectiveness. Two studies conducted by Good, Grouws, and Ebmeier (45) and Evertson, Emmer, and Brophy (34) found that mathematics teachers obtained more positive results when they taught the meaning of the concepts. Less positive results were found when mathematics teachers engaged in teaching other than concepts—for example, letting their students spend time working independently or on transitional activities such as solving problems (42).

Setting high expectations for all their students is another attribute of effective teachers. Research studies are unnecessary to tell teachers the obvious, but it needs to be stated: teacher expectations influence student performance. What seems to be significant is that these studies indicate that teacher expecta-

11

tions—a teacher's beliefs about a student's potential to learn—are communicated in subtle, yet well-defined ways.

Various research studies in the following areas have documented patterns of differential treatment that have produced expectancy effects (31):

- Length of time after questions (93, 94, 16)

- Efforts to assist students in their response (58, 3)

- Degree and frequency of praise and reinforcement (93, 94, 123, 119)

- Amounts of attention or nature of the interaction in groups and individually (43, 24)

- Proximity of teacher to students (86)

- Level of expectations (12)

- Degree of benefit of doubt on tests (50)

- Degree of eye contact (21)

- Use of classroom time (115, 42)

- Level of questioning (16)

Thus, the quality, frequency, and degree of student-teacher interactions can have a positive or negative effect on student learning. The research studies cited above are correlational and demonstrate "some of the consequences when teachers hold optimistic or pessimistic views of the learning potential of their pupils..." (31, p. 116). According to Ellson, a teacher's attitude can be "an important determinant of a pupil's performance" (31, p. 116).

There seems to be a strong relationship, then, between what a teacher expects and the resulting student performance, which is consistent with these expectations. This relationship is commonly known as the "self-fulfilling prophecy." Students often perform in ways that fulfill such a prophecy.

The point to stress is that teachers should establish expectations for all their students—not just the academically talented ones. In addition, secondary teachers should be aware that their verbal and nonverbal behaviors influence their students' responses. Therefore, it becomes the teacher's responsibility to vary instruction and to provide an environment that is conducive to learning for all students, not just a few.

Rosenshine (91) has given a detailed description of several teaching functions, citing recommendations for effective teaching and the supporting research studies. A discussion of five of these functions follows.

1. *Daily review of previous day's assignments.* For the intermediate grades this means beginning a class by checking homework, followed by a review of the previous day's work (44, 32).

2. *Presenting new content/skills.* Many teachers spend time demonstrating skills and concepts to their students, but research conducted in grades 4–8 found that effective mathematics teachers spend more time demonstrating than do ineffective ones. In fact, research (34, 44) has shown that effective teachers spend at least twenty-three minutes per day in lecturing, demonstrating, and discussing. In comparison, their less effective colleagues spend eleven minutes or less in such activities. During the lecture, demonstration, and discussion sequence, the effective teacher is providing explanations, using examples, and giving adequate instruction for seatwork. Demonstrations are a common part of instruction in English grammar, science, and foreign languages as well. Several recommendations that secondary teachers might find helpful, gleaned from experimental studies by Evertson, Emmer, and Brophy (34), and Kennedy, Bush, Cruickshank, and Haefele (64), are as follows:

a. Material (concepts, directions, etc.) should be organized in increments, in small steps, and each step mastered before going on.

b. As the material is presented, digressions should be avoided and the teacher should model the skill. If applicable, several examples should be cited and many varied explanations of difficult points should be offered.

c. Checking for understanding by asking questions is a prerequisite for moving to the next step.

d. Demonstrating the steps/process involved in how to answer higher-order questions (application, analysis, and synthesis) assists students in developing this skill.

3. *Guided student practice.* Correlational and experimental studies (111, 22, 112, 33) indicate that teachers who are effective ask a "pattern of factual questions-student response-teacher feedback" (91, p. 340). This pattern generally involves two types of questions—those that have a specific answer and those that require students to explain how they found the answer. Studies by Anderson et al. (4) and Good and Grouws (44) found that when the guided practice was followed by the question format, including consistent teacher feedback, student achievement was higher. Some guidelines that effective teachers followed are—

a. Calling on all students—those with their hands raised and those with their hands not raised

b. Writing down answers to questions and comparing them with those of other students

c. Summarizing and writing the main points on the board.

4. *Feedback and correctives.* Responding to and correcting student answers are other teaching functions that effective teachers use. There are a number of ways to respond to students when their answers are correct. For example, the teacher can reply in a positive manner ("Correct" or "Very good") and follow up quickly with a new question to keep the momentum of the lesson going (4). When students respond incorrectly, the teacher can offer hints, ask easier questions (112, 4), or reteach the material by providing additional examples (44, 78).

The main point is not to let the error go uncorrected. This does not, however, mean giving the student the right answer and moving on. Rather, teachers need to analyze student responses and be ready to provide the necessary remediation. Immediate feedback discourages students from developing habitual patterns of error and encourages them to learn from their mistakes.

5. *Independent practice.* Independent practice follows successful guided practice. When engaged in independent practice,

students are usually seated at their desks. For this engagement to be meaningful, teachers should prepare students for seatwork (33, 35), do the first problem together with them (4, 54), actively monitor students as they work with brief contacts (33, 35), and allow students to work with each other (97, 102, 103).

Rosenshine and Furst (92) also have identified nine process variables that are associated with effective instruction. These variables, too, have been correlated with student achievement:

1. Clarity of instruction
2. Explanation during instruction
3. Enthusiasm during instruction
4. Task orientation
5. Learning opportunities other than listening
6. Use of multiple levels of discourse
7. Use of student ideas
8. Use of noncritical remarks
9. Use of interesting questions.

The last area to focus on is student understanding and meaning. According to Barell (9), teaching thinking skills "stresses the search for meaning" (p. 18). Teachers help students "create meaning out of experience" (9, p. 18). Teachers have to lay the foundation for learning by encouraging students to build on what they have previously learned and experienced.

Barnes (10) cites several behaviors that teachers can use to promote the development of basic skills and higher-order thinking:

1. Varying the level of the questions asked
2. Probing, rephrasing, and prompting students
3. Waiting for a response
4. Providing answers to questions
5. Asking process-type questions (Tell me how you arrived at that answer?)
6. Stressing meaning and student understanding.

These six teacher behaviors can help teachers structure the instructional process in a way that helps students understand what they are learning.

SUMMARY

Effective teaching is made possible by studying effective teaching behaviors found in the literature and practiced in classrooms. We hope that secondary teachers will use the research on teacher effectiveness presented in this chapter as guidelines to analyze their own behavior and consider incorporating some of these attributes into their own teaching. In addition, as we present examples in the remaining part of this book, these attributes will also be evident. We hope they will encourage secondary teachers to think about the teaching act by asking questions, reflecting upon the answers, and proposing alternative solutions.

Chapter 2
THE TEACH-PRACTICE-APPLY MODEL

To help secondary teachers diversify their teaching repertoire, a structural framework with appropriate guidelines is necessary. As stated earlier, this text focuses on helping teachers acquire mastery of additional strategies. Appropriate guidelines usually appear as systems or models; several excellent models are currently in use. Among the more notable are Hunter's five-step instructional model (54), Joyce and Showers's coaching model (61), and Rosenshine's direct instruction model (90). In addition, expanding on Hunt's notion of flexibility, Joyce and Weil (62) compiled a comprehensive description of over twenty alternative teaching models.

While all these models have merit and have been used with degrees of success, we believe that they lack the conceptual simplicity necessary to help teachers effect change. Therefore we propose the Teach-Practice-Apply (TPA) model as an alternative that secondary teachers can use to augment their existing teaching strategies. This chapter begins with an overview of three general dimensions of secondary instruction—content, theory and strategies. Then it describes the TPA model in detail.

CONTENT, THEORY, AND STRATEGIES

Successful teaching depends largely on expertise in three dimensions of classroom instruction, broadly classified as knowledge of subject matter, knowledge of teaching and learning theory, and the selection and utilization of appropriate teaching strategies (27, 66, 71). Educational reformers and legislators recently have endorsed circumventing the traditional teacher certification program by encouraging those with a minimum of a baccalaureate degree to enter the teaching profession. According to Warner (122), four states—New Jersey, Florida, Texas, and Georgia—have made provisions for "alternative certification programs" that allow those with subject matter competency, but no pedagogical training, to teach.

17

A baccalaureate degree would seem to be sufficient to help meet the needs of the current and projected teacher shortages (26). But consider the following example. In the fall of 1964, the Chicago School District hired 1,000 liberal arts and science graduates; by the following spring only 167 had survived on the job (55). Because of the multidimensional demands placed on teachers, subject matter competency is usually not enough to retain qualified teachers in our secondary schools.

A solid foundation of learning theory (behaviorism, cognitive field, etc.) also is essential, as is knowledge of various teaching strategies. All teachers have experienced instructional situations, such as in-service sessions, in which the presenter understood the content but could not communicate it to those in the audience.

Neither is familiarity with teaching strategies alone sufficient for effective instruction. Secondary teachers often are encouraged to use resources beyond the text and those associated with it to enrich their teaching (80, 2). But in some cases teachers have not mastered the subject matter well enough to make full use of these resources.

Clearly, then, all three dimensions—content, learning theory, and strategies—are fundamental to good teaching. Recognizing the significance of all three, we assume that secondary teachers who make use of this text understand their subject matter and are familiar with the theoretical underpinnings of the teaching-learning process. It is the last dimension, strategies, that is emphasized in the remaining chapters.

TEACH-PRACTICE-APPLY (TPA)

The Teach-Practice-Apply approach is a form of direct instruction discussed by Cooper and others (25) in the context of teaching reading skills. While these researchers found the approach effective in reading instruction, it is also readily applicable to other curriculum areas. The following pages describe the steps of the TPA model as well as its application beyond reading to other secondary subjects. Although each step of the TPA model is considered separately, it should be noted that overlapping often occurs between the components. (See Figure 2.1 for an illustration of its overlapping nature.)

Figure 2.1
The Overlapping Nature of the Teach-Practice-Apply Model

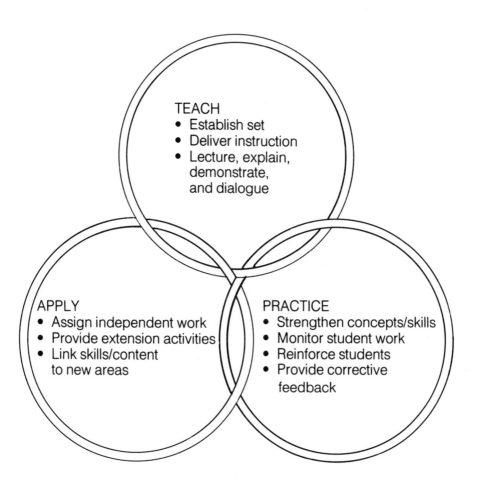

TEACH
• Establish set
• Deliver instruction
• Lecture, explain,
  demonstrate,
  and dialogue

APPLY
• Assign independent work
• Provide extension activities
• Link skills/content
  to new areas

PRACTICE
• Strengthen concepts/skills
• Monitor student work
• Reinforce students
• Provide corrective
  feedback

The Teach

Most instructional sessions should and do begin with a teach. This lesson component provides students with necessary information and/or skills. Its focus is on the teacher who uses media and materials, explains, and demonstrates while introducing the new concept. The purpose of the teach is to relate new information under study to the knowledge and skills from previous lessons and the students' experiential backgrounds. Lecturing, explaining, directing, demonstrating, and dialoguing are often associated with the systematic instruction that occurs during the teach. Accompanying the use of these techniques, other teacher skills such as organization, clarity of instruction, enthusiasm, and student interaction come into play to create a mindset for learning.

Used at the beginning of a lesson, the teach introduces concepts and/or skills that help students develop a level of understanding necessary for successful completion of the exercises and assignments in the practice and apply components. The brief example that follows illustrates how a student teacher, using maps, failed to provide appropriate instruction before initiating a practice activity.

A student teacher, responsible for teaching basic map skills in a junior high social studies class, asked students to account for the total number of rivers, lakes, and mountains on the map. "When you are done look to the front, and if you have a question raise your hand." He introduced neither the map symbols for the requested features nor their usage on the face and in the legend of the map. Consequently, the students could not identify or count these features with certainty. In effect, without instruction about the map symbols and their meanings, the practice assignment was premature; it therefore confused rather than facilitated the students' comprehension of the new information.

The duration of the teach component will vary. For a teacher using a demonstration strategy, it will be relatively lengthy; for a teacher using cooperative learning or gaming strategies, it will be relatively brief because more time will be allocated for the practice and the apply components.

The Practice

The second lesson component provides students with opportunities to "practice" what has been presented in the teach. During the practice, students engage in activities that are directly related to the essential concepts and/or skills presented. The practice component of TPA shifts the emphasis away from the teacher to the students. Careful monitoring of activities ensures that each student is carrying out the assigned task and thus reflecting an understanding of the concept or skill practiced.

In the example cited, during the teach the student teacher should first have introduced the language of map symbols and conventions. Next, he should have related the symbolization on maps to previous instruction and to the students' experiential backgrounds by demonstrating the logic of conventions, such as the consistent use of the color blue to designate rivers, lakes, and other bodies of water. Then, the student teacher would have established a mindset for learning. Finally, he should have elicited responses to questions about features on various maps before asking each student to count the rivers, lakes, and mountains on the handout map.

Students may misunderstand concepts or they may practice skills incorrectly. Consequently, the role of the teacher during the practice component must be an active one. He/she must monitor practice activities, be prepared to intervene when students are having difficulty, and use positive reinforcement when the concepts and skills are being demonstrated successfully. Although this latter aspect of the teacher's role is particularly important, as Goodlad (46) points out, often it is conspicuously absent.

The Apply

Once students have demonstrated a basic grasp of the concepts or skills, the teacher must provide more challenging and creative activities that require them to apply what they have learned to related areas and in a broader context. In the apply component, students are expected and encouraged to work independently and to demonstrate their comprehension of the desired concepts or skills. In the social studies example used, the students could be assigned to draw their own maps of a specified region designating the various features. Further, they could create their own symbolic language for these maps and the designation of these features. Then, they might write a justification stressing the logical connections between their symbols and their use and the geographic reality. These learning opportunities allow students to more fully understand the nature of maps and their content as well as to go beyond the maps into the broader realm of graphic expression.

It is helpful to consider homework assignments as part of the application component of the lesson, since by definition homework occurs outside the classroom and without any direct supervision by the teacher. Therefore, as with all activities within each TPA component, homework assignments require the teacher's careful consideration to achieve the desired lesson outcomes. So, too, with testing. The construction of tests that require higher-order thinking is a serious undertaking, which should be of particular interest to secondary teachers. Creative testing not only elicits students' knowledge of the desired subject matter or skills, but it also can challenge them to apply what they have learned.

THE TPA OVERLAP, SPIRAL, RETEACH

There are two characteristics inherent in the Teach-Practice-Apply model. The first, as stated earlier, is that the TPA components overlap. Consequently, there is an element of practice in both the teach and apply components. Similarly, a good teach will include aspects of the other components. Figure 2.1 illustrates this overlap.

The second characteristic of the Teach-Practice-Apply model is a spiraling effect. (See Figure 2.2.) Bruner (18) advocated a spiral curriculum in which basic concepts are presented with greater complexity and sophistication at each higher grade level. Ausubel's (6) advance organizer concept is also based on the premise that instruction at any level should be related to underlying, supporting concepts, facts, and skills. So, too, with Barron's graphic organizer, which he called the structured overview (11). The TPA model is congruent with the ideas of Bruner, Ausubel, and Barron. For example:

22

Figure 2.2
The Spiral Nature of the Teach-Practice-Apply Model*

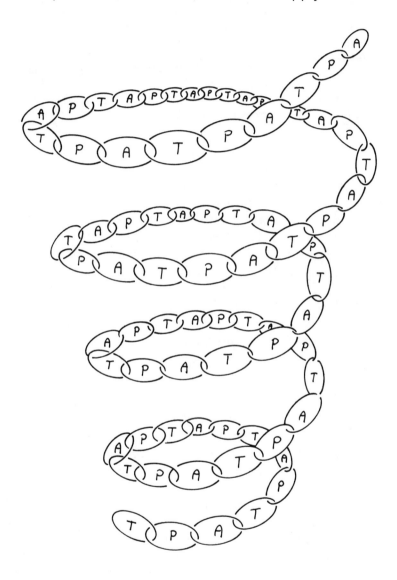

*T = Teach　　　P = Practice　　　A = Apply

In a tenth grade biology class the teacher asks students to identify the basic characteristics of some sample angiosperms (flowering plants). Building on their previous knowledge of plant reproduction, the students now have an opportunity to practice by focusing on the fruit and flowers and examining these parts. Once the fruit and the flower parts are dissected, the students are ready to apply their new knowledge in a discussion about the process of fertilization. From an understanding of how angiosperms reproduce, generalizations can be made as an introduction to a future lesson on animal reproduction.

Should students experience difficulty at one level, teachers can modify the activities to reteach the concept or skill before moving to the next level. (See Figure 2.3.) A reteach step can be implemented quickly. Teachers recognize that reteaching is needed by constantly monitoring the practice and application components of the lesson. When a reteach is necessary, teachers should first reassess the student's attitude, learning mode, and the instructional setting, as well as the difficulty level of the task. Then, using different examples and teaching strategies, they reteach a concept/skill/technique.

SUMMARY

The Teach-Practice-Apply model is a paradigm that retains the best of direct instruction while allowing the teacher the flexibility necessary to use a variety of deductive and inductive instructional strategies (84). Its emphasis is on the application of knowledge—not merely "knowing" it.

Although the TPA components are sequenced, the emphasis and time provided for each component vary with the differing teaching strategies used and the concepts developed. For example, a deductive lesson would have considerably more time allocated to the teach portion, while an inductive activity would have more time allocated to the practice portion.

Figure 2.3
A Reteach Loop

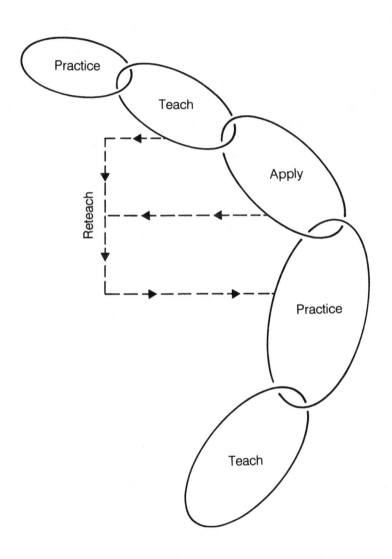

Chapter 3
DIRECT INSTRUCTION: LECTURE AND TEACHER DEMONSTRATION

DESCRIPTION

While the lecture method may no longer be fashionable, it remains one of the most effective forms of instruction because it is predicated upon direct communication between teacher and students. It also has been tried, tested, and perfected over several millennia. The lecture method first became a standard instructional strategy in the Bronze Age when it was skillfully employed by such master teachers as Confucius. It proved extremely effective during the Middle Ages when it was at the core of the humanistic teaching-learning process. And it was introduced into the United States in the first half of the nineteenth century by such brilliant lecturers as historian George Bancroft as part of the great education reform emanating from the German universities.

In the literature today, the lecture is often referred to as direct instruction (90, 65). The basic premises of direct instruction are very similar to those of the lecture: (1) it is used with large groups, (2) it is teacher-directed, and (3) its focus is academic content (72). Despite recent rather ruthless attacks in the name of reform, innovation, and relevancy, the lecture remains a mainstay of American secondary education. Indeed, research has not shown it to be less effective (79). The fault is not with the lecture method, but with its implementation by practitioners. It is not necessarily for everyone, nor is it a universal panacea.

An effective lecturer does not talk at an audience. Effective lecturing is a highly personalized human strategy that conveys not only information, but inspiration and emotion. In so doing it arouses, motivates, and allows for human reactions and responses—irritation, confusion, attention—from the audience. An effective lecturer is a great communicator who directly involves an audience. This method, especially when coupled with teacher demonstrations, offers a high degree of flexibility to recapitulate, clarify, explore, and emphasize. And it is cost-effective.

The lecture method, in combination with demonstrations, encourages teachers and students to interact verbally and nonverbally as they raise questions, observe specific techniques, and listen to the give-and-take of the lesson. "When teachers explain exactly what students are expected to learn, and demonstrate the steps needed to accomplish a particular academic task, students learn more" (13, p. 35).

For us, the lecture method with teacher demonstration is a form of direct instruction. Direct instruction is teacher-centered. "It provides students with opportunities to observe the teacher modeling skills and then allows them time to practice and apply these skills" (84, p. 43). Combining lecture and demonstration is more than merely telling students and showing them, however. Beyond a subject matter knowledge base, this strategy takes commitment, "a fair amount of foresight and organization to help anyone learn anything from a lecture" (77). In addition, it takes careful execution on the part of the teacher. Before beginning the lecture, the teacher provides the objectives and uses key words (clues during the presentation-demonstration) to correlate objectives to statements made during the presentation (72, 77).

Two assumptions underlie the lecture-demonstration strategy: (1) not all students know how to learn and (2) instruction and assignments are broken down into small, systematic steps. When selecting this instructional strategy, Reinhartz (81) offers teachers six points to consider:

1. Teaching students how to listen, see, and question to get them more involved in the lecture
2. Practicing listening and observing skills yourself
3. Showing students how to take notes during oral presentations—what information to record, the proper form for notes, their collation and storage, how to use them for tests and other written exercises
4. Ways of getting and holding students' attention by establishing set, linking new information with that previously learned, and using multisensory aids. A review at the beginning of each class of the previous day's material gets them thinking about the topic.

27

5. Behaviors to use during the lecture demonstration:
   —Using voice level to emphasize points
   —Interjecting humorous stories/anecdotes
   —Moving around the room while talking
   —Asking questions periodically to check for understanding and to determine how well students are listening
   —Asking students to paraphrase what has been said
   —Bringing closure to the topic
6. Using advance organizers and structured overviews to emphasize major concepts and to provide continuity from lesson to lesson. Advance organizers or their graphic counterparts may be put on the board for all to see.

A general rule of thumb to keep in mind when preparing a lecture-demonstration is to spend 20 percent of the time telling students what they will be told and shown, 60 percent telling and showing them, and another 20 percent summarizing what they have been told and have seen. Following the steps outlined for the lecture-demonstration, teachers help students get organized for learning. It is also important to remember that an effective lecture-demonstration is not just "telling and showing, it is not a one-way process." Figure 3.1 provides a guide for preparing a lecture-demonstration.

LECTURE-TEACHER DEMONSTRATION AND TPA

When using the lecture-demonstration with TPA, the teacher assumes an especially dynamic role throughout the lesson—as planner, organizer, executor, and assessor, but at no time are students merely passive bystanders. While the teach is the dominant component, never are the students uninvolved. During the teach, the teacher not only tells students what is going to happen and carries out the lecture-demonstration, but also instigates student participation by getting them to take notes, to answer and ask questions, and otherwise to react to the presentation.

During the practice component the teacher helps students move from being the reactors to becoming the main actors.

Figure 3.1
Guide for Preparing a Lecture-Demonstration

When using the lecture-demonstration strategy—

1. the topic should be clearly defined for students.

2. the continuity of the topic should be clearly evident and related to topics that students have studied and will study.

3. emphasize the key concepts and essential information
   a. by restating them.
   b. by providing enough examples.
   c. by using advance organizers or structured overviews.

4. present the information
   a. reasonably and confidently.
   b. with humor and anecdotes.

5. actively involve students in the presentation by
   a. asking questions.
   b. having students take notes.
   c. having students anticipate what will come next.
   d. having students extrapolate.
   e. having students paraphrase.
   f. having students make comparisons and identify relationships.
   g. having students summarize and draw conclusions.

Through the insertion of stories/anecdotes, for example, students can be encouraged to relate what they know or have previously learned. Asking thought-provoking questions during the presentation can elicit student examples related to the topic. Sometimes, skillfully urging students to anticipate what is to come in the lecture-demonstration is good practice too—it can initiate application of their learning.

Asking students to address issues or concepts that have been broached directly or even peripherally during the presentation, orally and/or in writing, individually or in groups, is one way to have them apply their learning. Having them devise and deliver alternative demonstrations or minipresentations on the same or a related topic is another application. Gradually, from the teach through the practice to the apply, the centrality of the teacher is replaced by the centrality of the student, but neither is ever totally absent.

EXAMPLES

English

A high school English literature class is studying the development of the novel. As background, the teacher selects one class period to lecture on the topic "Coffeehouse England and the Birth of the Novel." The purpose of the presentation is to help students understand how the intellectual fermentation and interaction, particularly among the English literati of the late seventeenth and early eighteenth centuries, emanating from the rather unique institution of the coffeehouse helped give rise to the first examples of the modern novel in England. While providing the intellectual, social, and economic milieu for the birth of the novel, the lecture also will connect previous lessons on prenovel forms of literature, some of which students have read (e.g., *Journal of The Plague Year*, published by Daniel Defoe in 1722), to the lessons to come and to the example(s) of early novels students are about to read (e.g., *The Vicar of Wakefield*, published by Oliver Goldsmith in 1766).

In preparation for the lecture, the teacher has thoroughly researched not only the origins of the novel, but also the social, intellectual, and economic history of England and Western Europe in the late seventeenth and early eighteenth centuries. The teacher's outline reflects an understanding of both the literary foundations and the historical situation. So, for example, the teacher will be able to explain how the growth of the English overseas empire and trade led to a rise in coffee consumption (and a corresponding drop in alcohol consumption) and the founding of over five hundred coffeehouses in London by the reign of Queen Anne (1702-1707), and how, consequently, these establishments became social centers for representatives of the ever-more literate and aware members of the rising English middle class.

At the outset of the presentation, the teacher writes advance organizers such as Jonathan Swift, *Pamela*, British East India Company on the chalkboard. These might be accompanied by a display of readily available copies of period prints of London coffeehouses, Robinson Crusoe, etc. Correspondingly, the lecture can be interspersed with contemporary quotations from notables like Robert Hooke, Samuel Pepys, or Samuel Johnson commenting on the coffeehouse, London, or the British empire and trade. These period testimonials might also provide the bases for questions to encourage students to recall what they have learned or to anticipate the novel they will read.

Throughout the presentation, the teacher acts and reacts confidently with flexibility to students' questions. One specific application of what is being learned might be to ask students to compare in writing the social role of coffee today to its social role in the period under study. Do "coffeehouses" still exist today? If so, how are they similar to and/or different from those in the immediate and/or more distant past? Are they still intellectual gathering places? Do other social institutions today have similar functions and outcomes? Another application might be to ask students to discuss the role of intellectual interaction throughout history among more contemporary literary artists (e.g., "Beat poets") creating new literary forms or genres (e.g., science fiction).

Math

Using a topic from geometry, angles and their measurement, the teacher develops an elaborate lecture-demonstration. After the teacher explains what angles are and demonstrates how to measure them during the teach, the students practice constructing and measuring obtuse, acute, and right angles using a protractor.

A common statement teachers often hear from students is why they need to know about angles when they will never use the knowledge. During the apply component of the lesson, the teacher attempts to answer this question. Career application is one possible avenue. For example, Mary Ann is an architect who is designing buildings throughout the city of Austin, Texas. Interested in collecting solar energy for heating and cooling these buildings, she decides to use solar collectors. To save money, these solar collectors need to be at a fixed angle. What information does she need to determine the optimum heating angle?

The city: Austin, Texas
The latitude is 30°

Heating angle = latitude + 15°
             = 30° + 15°
             = 45°

Heating and cooling angle
= latitude + 5°
= 30° + 5
= 35

The teacher could also provide latitudes for other cities to be used for the same purposes. For example:

Miami, Florida—latitude 26°
Honolulu, Hawaii—latitude 21°

The same idea of career applications of geometry can be used with other occupations/professions such as design engineering, photography, mountain climbing, art, advertising, carpentry, navigation, and mineralogy.

SUMMARY

Lecture and demonstration, a form of direct instruction, structures learning so that it can be used with large groups to teach academic content. When using direct instruction, teachers convey more than content, however: they convey inspiration and emotion, they model skills, they communicate the lesson objectives, and they provide opportunities for students to practice and apply what they have learned and observed. They also carefully organize the statements they will make and identify the examples they will use to illustrate their main points.

In addition, teachers divide the lesson into small, systematic units that emphasize major skills and key concepts and provide continuity from class to class. As they implement direct instruction, teachers continually monitor student understanding and seek to involve students in the class presentation. Finally, teacher lecture-demonstration remains one of the most effective forms of instruction because it relies on direct interaction with students.

Applying Your Knowledge

1. The topic of your lecture is the Nature of Energy. Develop an outline to present this topic to your students. Here is a start:

Advance Organizers

1. There are several different forms of energy.
2. Energy cannot be converted, created, or destroyed.
3. Work, power, and energy are interrelated.
4.
5.
6.

Outline
   I. What is energy?

     A. Work
       1. Factors that determine work
       2. Examples to demonstrate work:
          a.
          b.

     B. Definition of Power

     C. Definition of energy
       1. Measuring energy
       2. Kinds of energy
          a. Potential
             (1) Elastic potential energy
             (2) Gravitational
             (3) What demonstration(s) will you use?
          b. Kinetic
          c. Examples
             (1)
             (2)

   II. Forms of energy

     A.
     B.
     C.
     D.
     E.

III. Conversion of energy
  A. Spontaneous reactions
     1.
     2.
  B. Nonspontaneous reactions
     1.
     2.
  C. Energy chain
     1.
     2.
  D. Examples of converting energy from one form to the other
     1. Visual for overhead or chalkboard

     Example: Energy changes form: electricity
     Coal ⟶ water to steam ⟶ steam turns
     (chemical)   (heat)
     turbines ⟶ turbines run generators ⟶ energy
     (mechanical)   (mechanical)   (electrical)
     2.
     3.

     (What demonstrations will you use to "show" how these examples are using the principle of converting one energy type into another?)
IV. History of energy
  A. James Joule (1840)
     1.
     2.
  B. Law of conservation of energy
     1. Einstein (1905)—$E = MC^2$
     2.
     3.
        (Demonstration planned)
  C. Past
     1.
     2.
     3.
  D. Present
     1.
     2.
     3.

E. Future
   1.
   2.
   3.

V. Energy supply
   1.
   2.
   3.
   4.

VI. Researching for new energy sources and their feasibility
   1.
   2.
   3.
   (Demonstrations planned)

VII. Global energy problems
   1.
   2.
   3.
   4. Examples:

2. Construct a "quadrilateral tree" (C. Miller and H. Vern, *Mathematical Ideas* [1978], Glenview, Ill.: Scott, Foresman Co., p. 295) as a means for preparing for the teach, practice, apply for geometry: polygons.

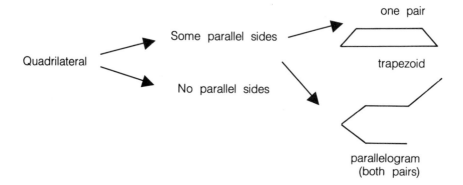

35

Analysis Guide for Direct Instruction:
Lecture and Teacher Demonstration

Did (I) the teacher—	Yes	No	N/A
1. select and define a unified manageable topic?	—	—	—
2. fully understand where the topic fits into the scheme of what students have learned and are learning?	—	—	—
3. fully research the topic?	—	—	—
4. identify learning objectives?	—	—	—
5. have in writing (or in outline form) the content to be presented?	—	—	—
6. identify what skills will be demonstrated?	—	—	—
7. develop and share advance organizers and/or develop a structured overview?	—	—	—
8. secure students' attention?	—	—	—
9. review previous day's material?	—	—	—
10. interject humor into the lecture?	—	—	—
11. use several examples to illustrate key points?	—	—	—
12. use key verbal clues to emphasize important information?	—	—	—
13. observe students to be sure they are practicing and applying the skills correctly and appropriately?	—	—	—
14. seek to involve the audience in the presentation?	—	—	—

Chapter 4
CONCEPT ATTAINMENT

DESCRIPTION

Concept attainment attempts to help students think. It forces students to group or categorize data based on specific criteria. Then, students are asked to provide labels to like information or events and disparate information. Giving labels to concepts actively involves students in the learning process. For Bruner (20), classifying information has two components: the act of concept formation and the actual identification of the concept.

Joyce and Weil (63) discuss variations on this teaching strategy. The focus in this chapter is on the Reception Model of concept attainment. This variation teaches students the characteristics of the concept in a direct instruction fashion. It is an inductive approach to learning in which the teacher presents positive and negative examples related to a particular concept. After a concept attainment exercise, students "discover" the concept. By engaging in the three steps of the strategy—(1) identifying and sequencing the characteristics of the concept, (2) selecting positive and negative examples, and (3) analyzing the concept—students learn what concepts are and how to acquire them.

There are two advantages of using concept attainment: (1) it is appropriate for all grade levels and ages, and (2) it requires minimal resources and effort. The only requirement is that the teacher plan ahead in order to have an array of sequenced examples (63) that are alike and different in some ways.

Concept attainment is more than a guessing exercise. To be successful and to avoid guessing, teachers need to employ a systematic approach that involves planning. Concept learning draws on extensive research; therefore it might be helpful to keep the following in mind when implementing this strategy. Every concept has (1) a name; (2) both positive and negative examples that can be used to describe it; (3) characteristics, qualities, and attributes; and (4) a rule that can be used to define it.

Concept attainment also uses a particular vocabulary, including *examples, positive and negative,* and *attributes.* These terms are part of the language Bruner and his associates use to explain the instructional strategy. The purpose of concept learning, then, is to help students differentiate between the examples and nonexamples. For Bruner, the real test is to have students distinguish between characteristics that are not critical and those that are.

Concept attainment is an effective strategy to use to establish a mindset for new learning or to get students to summarize the diverse information they have received during a lecture or while researching a topic. Helping students see that a specific combination of characteristics sets one concept apart from another is the key to the use of this strategy. For example, consider an apple and a grapefruit and their shape—both are round, but they possess other distinguishing qualities such as taste, texture (skin, meat), color, juiciness.

The first step, the planning phase, is to identify and sequence the characteristics or attributes of the concept under investigation. The second step is to carefully select the positive examples that have all the essential attributes of the concept (63). The examples can be a single word, a symbol, or a phrase. The nonexamples should make it difficult to determine the concept. Whether the strategy is used to introduce a new concept, to expand a present concept, or to summarize a concept, the type of positive and negative examples presented is essential. During the second step, students should focus on the examples and nonexamples and the discussion generated from their contributions. The final phase of the second step is to formulate hypotheses to try to identify the concept.

Once the concept has been identified, the third step begins with analyzing it. Analysis requires students to review the groupings of examples and nonexamples to determine relationships and patterns (63). This analysis is the heart of concept attainment. Based on subsequent examples and nonexamples, hypotheses are discarded and/or modified. Identification of the concept in step two, although significant, is a by-product of the type of thinking the student experiences during concept learning.

Concept attainment can be used with the whole class with students individually participating in the process, or it can be designed as a small group activity. For best results, it is recommended that teachers begin with a large group; when students become familiar with the steps, teachers can use concept attainment with smaller groups.

In the Reception Model briefly described, the teacher is in control of the concept, the examples used, and the sequence used in their presentation. If one views instructional strategies as a continuum, concept attainment as presented is an extension of direct instruction. The form that concept attainment takes is determined by the teacher's objective, what he/she hopes to accomplish by using this strategy and concept-building skills. In the beginning the teacher should be in greater control of the concept attainment process. When smaller groups are used, however, students structure the process and determine the examples and the order of their introduction.

CONCEPT ATTAINMENT AND TPA

The Teach-Practice-Apply format is compatible with the concept attainment strategy. According to Reinhartz and Van Cleaf (85), "the teacher assumes direct responsibility for the lesson..." by presenting positive and negative examples and directions for proceeding (p. 35). For example:

Rather than defining what decimal fractions are, the teacher writes pairs of fractions on the chalkboard:

Positive Examples			Negative Examples	
$\dfrac{2}{10}$	$\dfrac{5}{100}$		$\dfrac{8}{16}$	$\dfrac{1}{2}$
$\dfrac{10}{1000}$	$\dfrac{1}{100}$		$\dfrac{5}{25}$	$\dfrac{1}{5}$
$\dfrac{11}{100}$	$\dfrac{23}{100}$		$\dfrac{11}{22}$	$\dfrac{1}{2}$

The practice occurs when students analyze and interpret each example and proceed to categorize the data into some type of scheme. In the previous example, the students determine the common feature of the positive examples and determine why the negative examples do not share this common feature. Students have an opportunity to expand their thinking as they become actively engaged with the data (117). Throughout the practice, the teacher poses eliciting questions. These questions propel students into concept formation and data analysis by getting them to relate similar and dissimilar features. Discussing the thought processes used to determine the concept, decimal fractions, brings the practice to a close.

The apply activities build on the teach (presentation of examples and questions) and practice (analysis and interpretation of data and formulating hypotheses). Here, students are asked to determine how decimal fractions relate to other fractions—for example, equivalent fractions. After analyzing positive and negative examples, students find that decimal fractions have denominators of 10, 100, 1000, etc., while other fractions do not necessarily have such denominators. Also, equivalent fractions are the same as (equal with) a fraction that is in its lowest terms, but whose denominator is not necessarily a power of ten. For example: $2/16 = 1/8$. But decimal fractions can be equivalent fractions—for example: $20/100 = 1/5$. In other words, decimal fractions can be equivalent fractions, but not all equivalent fractions are decimal fractions.

ADDITIONAL EXAMPLES

Government

The primary objective in a high school government course is for students to derive an understanding of Soviet Communism. After careful research and planning, the teacher prepared the following list of positive and negative examples.

Positive Examples	Negative Examples
economic system	economic competition
social system	individualism
political system	popular sovereignty
V. I. Lenin	Thomas Jefferson
Russian Revolution	American Revolution
totalitarian dictatorship	republican democracy
welfare state	private property

From a teacher-directed discussion *comparing and contrasting* the positive and negative examples, the students are to conceptualize and identify the objective—Soviet Communism. ("V. I. Lenin" and

"Russian Revolution" should be the giveaway and/or confirmation!)

During the practice component when students analyze the examples, a secondary objective is achieved. Students are not only delineating Soviet Communism, but they are comparing and contrasting it with American Capitalism! The practice can then lead naturally to applying what they have learned in a more elaborate discussion or a composition about the two systems, their similarities and their differences. For example, both are born of revolutions based on ideologies deeply rooted in the mainstream of Western tradition, but with very different outcomes. A further application can be to ask students to try to account for these different outcomes. Among the possible factors to consider are Russia's Eurasian heritage, Russia's historic isolation from the West, classical Marxism vs. Marxism-Leninism-Stalinism, and the nature of the Russian Revolution. One additional benefit of this lesson will be that throughout, students will be challenged not only to recall, but to reconsider, what they have learned previously about the American system.

Geography/Ecology

A high school geography class is examining the long-term impact of humans on the environment. The teacher wants students to realize that this impact is not necessarily detrimental to the environment or to humans; to do so she decides to present the case for the development of a multiple-purpose river basin. She writes the following examples on the board:

Positive Examples	Negative Examples
dams and canals	natural state
hydroelectric energy	wild river
irrigation and flood control	flooding
commerce	erosion
water supply	siltation
recreation	drought
wildlife management	water pollution

Through a consideration of the examples, guided by the teacher, students achieve the concept of environmental management with regard to rivers. During this discussion students are encouraged to cite specific examples. Thus, the Colorado River as it runs through the Grand Canyon might be considered both in its "natural state" and also "wild river" at times. At the same time, the Hoover Dam across the Colorado between Nevada and Arizona creates a classic multiple-purpose river basin development experience.

In analyzing the examples students put in practice what they are

41

learning. They will come to realize that environmental management and development, despite its apparent benefits, may not always be desirable. Often there are very good reasons for leaving segments of the natural environment alone.

In the apply component students can be asked individually or in groups, orally or in writing, to make the case for or against selectively altering the environment and to provide more local or international case studies. Similarly, the teacher also can assign students to develop their own lists of examples for other geographical features (e.g., deserts) and their development and/or preservation by humans.

SUMMARY

The concept attainment strategy described in this chapter helps students process information in a way that encourages them to learn and retain it. There is evidence to suggest that students learn and retain information better (more efficiently) when they have opportunities to organize it conceptually. Listing positive and negative examples helps to classify information as it is being presented. Concept formulation using the clues given through the examples forces students to engage in higher-order thinking and to transfer newly acquired concepts to new information. This allows students to generalize beyond the current situation. Using the concept attainment strategy, then, is effective across content areas and age groups as students formulate abstract ideas in an attempt to understand specific information and to determine meanings. "It is meaning in this sense that allows the student to exercise the powers of inference, self-understanding, and thoughtful action" (77, p. 25).

Applying Your Knowledge

I. Develop a concept attainment lesson for green plants and nongreen plants.

A. *Positive Examples*   *Negative Examples*
   1. Chlorophyl   1.
   2.   2.
   3.   3.
   4.   4.
   5.   5.

B. Students formulate the concept under investigation
   1. Analyze the data
   2. Interpret information
   3.
   4.

C. Discussion of thought processes and of each example

II. Develop a concept attainment activity for binomial distribution—to identify if an experiment is Bernoulli or not.

A. *Positive Examples*   *Negative Examples*
   1. Toss of a coin   1.
      (heads or tails)
   2. Firecrackers   2.
      (explode or are duds)
   3.   3.
   4.   4.
   5.   5.

B. Analysis of examples

C. Discussion

Analysis Guide
for Concept Attainment

Did (I) the teacher—	Yes	No	N/A
1. identify an appropriate concept?	___	___	___
2. provide appropriate positive examples?	___	___	___
3. provide appropriate negative examples?	___	___	___
4. present examples in a logical and appropriate sequence?	___	___	___
5. ask students to describe the thought processes they used to analyze and interpret the examples provided?	___	___	___
6. ask students how each positive example related to the concept and how each negative example did not?	___	___	___
7. get students to extend and apply the concept beyond the current context and discussions?	___	___	___

Chapter 5
GUIDED DISCUSSION

DESCRIPTION

Controversial issues come to mind when the instructional strategy, discussion, is mentioned. Members of discussion groups often ponder a question or a problem and begin to think about solutions. They begin to think about how they really feel about the question or problem and to decide if they have an opinion. According to Hoover and Hollingsworth (52), the discussion method is ideal for "evolving, sorting, and sifting facts and values essential for the resolution of problems" (p. 114). It is also suitable for achieving cognitive as well as affective goals.

For Joyce and Weil (62), the discussion parallels the group investigation model because it shares many common properties. There is, for example, a respect for ideas and a commitment to inquiry and group interaction. In this chapter, however, the discussion strategy is presented in more universal terms.

First of all, the discussion strategy is not a group of students chatting or being told to do their assignment in preparation for a discussion. The latter scenario dissolves into responding to low-level questions; it is merely a question-answer session with the teacher leading students. Why and when do teachers select a discussion strategy? Most teachers select a discussion because it increases interaction between teacher and students and among students. Through this interaction, students use process skills that encourage them to state their opinions, to talk to each other, and to articulate their particular points of view. Some may call it brainstorming, an inquiry group, or a buzz group. But guided discussion is different. It has structure, with emphasis on both the process and the product; the goal is not necessarily to achieve a consensus, nor for the teacher necessarily to function as the chief questioner or responder. The discussion strategy allows, and, most importantly, encourages students to think critically and to talk to each other. However, the leadership of the teacher and a broad academic ability are required for successful conduct of a guided discussion.

An inherent characteristic of the discussion strategy is that it allows and encourages the free exchange of ideas. It is less teacher-directed than the previously described strategies—direct instruction and concept attainment. An effective discussion should also consider the following (81):

1. The arrangement of furniture to enhance interaction (half circle, circle format)
2. The classroom rules for acceptable behavior that all students are to follow during a discussion
3. The use of verbal and nonverbal behaviors to encourage student responses
4. The teacher's position and role during the discussion (varying his/her position in the group, referring questions to the group, and refraining from approving or disapproving of responses, for example).

The role of the teacher employing the discussion method becomes that of facilitator rather than of director. As facilitator the teacher promotes learning through the exchange of ideas and points of view, facts, and opinions as students interact. At first glance, planning may not seem necessary for a successful discussion. Yet closer examination makes it apparent that planning is indeed necessary to ensure that students are motivated; that questions are prepared in advance to promote free interaction among students, as well as the use of cognitive skills (analysis, synthesis, and evaluation). In other words, the teacher needs to be organized and ready to implement a carefully thought-out plan. The discussion itself tests the plan; that is, the success or failure of the discussion can point to areas of the plan that need modification. Successive discussions also retest the plan.

Discussions are designed to teach a particular principle or generalization; they are less effective for teaching specific content (57). However, students can learn, practice, and apply skills by participating in a discussion. For example, they can learn the give-and-take of a discussion, practice active listening, handle controversy, and develop leadership ability.

As teachers prepare for a discussion, they must make at least *five* decisions (see Figure 5.1). First, they must determine the goals to be accomplished in order to make these clear to their

46

Figure 5.1
Five Decisions Teachers Make
to Prepare for a Discussion

1. Identify the goals to be accomplished.

2. Determine the format (whole class/small group) for the discussion.

3. Provide specific directions to carry out the discussion.

4. Determine the amount of time to be allotted to the discussion.

5. Determine the product that will result from the discussion.

students. For example, if the goal is the acquisition of a skill, which one will it be—to develop leadership, listening, and/or paraphrasing skill? Second, the teacher must determine the format for the discussion. Will it take place with the entire class or in small groups? Will it be led by the teacher or by the students? Goal setting will help determine the format.

The third decision deals with directions. How detailed they will be will depend upon the age of the group, the level of experience, and the goal(s). The fourth decision, the allotment of an appropriate amount of time, is crucial because small groups tend to fill the time with everything but the topic to be discussed. The fifth decision concerns the type of product that students should prepare based on the discussion—list the conclusions, graph the results, make a table. This product can be used to make final comments to group members.

As part of the planning and decision-making process, the teacher needs to determine several procedural issues as well (52). For example, identifying the type of problem to focus on is vital, whether it deals with the evaluation of factual information, values, advocacy, or policy. The issues discussed help classify the type of problem selected.

Once the directions have been given and the type of problem has been decided upon, the next step in the process is to analyze

47

the problem. In this phase students determine the important terms and facts related to the problem. Once the problem components have been analyzed, hypotheses need to be established. Formulating hypotheses provides students with possible alternatives to solve the problem. From among the many hypotheses, they derive generalizations.

Lastly, the teacher needs to prepare for the role of facilitator or discussion leader. Asking focusing, closure-seeking, and probing questions, paraphrasing comments, writing key information on the board, and remaining nonjudgmental are skills the discussion leader needs in order to encourage students to be open-minded, flexible, objective, and reflective concerning the problem under investigation. Another necessary skill is that of handling the dynamics of a group setting.

In addition to making the many decisions involved in planning for a discussion, the teacher needs to instruct students in the characteristics inherent in this teaching strategy—for example, receptivity to new ideas and objectivity. Before entering into a discussion, all students need to examine their individual biases. This examination process helps participants recognize that everyone is coming from a somewhat different perspective and that the object is not to change a person's mind, but to be tolerant enough to accept different opinions. Another characteristic of the discussion is objectivity. It is important that students engage in the process by accepting ideas on their own merits. Once the teacher deals with open-mindedness and objectivity, the discussion is ready to begin.

At the conclusion of the discussion, teacher and students need to be prepared to evaluate the goals, the procedure, and the performance of participants through self- and group ratings. The evaluation process should focus on preplanning by the teacher, the questions, the information initially presented, the actual face-to-face exchange of ideas, the level of participation, the nature and quality of the contributions, the degree of group cohesion, the conclusions reached concerning the topic under discussion, and the attainment of the goal(s).

GUIDED DISCUSSION AND TPA

Teachers who decide to diversify their repertoire by using a guided discussion will find that it can work well within the TPA paradigm. When this strategy is used with the TPA model, the teach is both the dominant and the continuous component. It begins with the decision to use a guided discussion and continues with the careful planning needed to orchestrate the discussion to achieve the content and skill objectives sought. Special attention must be given to the framing of questions to initiate, stimulate, and facilitate the projected discussion.

For example, a high school social studies teacher wants students to achieve some understanding of the complex relationships that exist between subcultures ("minorities") and the superculture ("the majority") in the United States. At the same time students will be encouraged to examine their personal biases vis-à-vis specific subcultures. To initiate and stimulate the discussion, the teacher employs a "reading your neighborhood" approach (84) by projecting a slide of a Hispanic "barrio mural" on the wall of the classroom. After allowing enough time for the class to experience the mural, the teacher initiates the discussion with a series of questions. "What is most striking about the mural?" (color, subject matter, symbols, mood, etc.) "Why do these aspects stand out?" (strangeness, alien to the superculture) "What do they tell us?" (alienation)

In a guided discussion the practice phase is the discussion itself, but the teach continues with the teacher's role shifting from leader to facilitator. Thus, through guidance and periodic intervention by referring to the mural, which remains projected on the wall throughout the discussion, the teacher facilitates the learning of content and the practicing of skills while helping students know themselves better by having them examine some of their prejudices.

During the apply component, the teacher asks students to evaluate the discussion, its content, and their respective roles. In the process, students also carry out appraisals of themselves. To further apply what they have learned, the teacher might require each student to construct a personal mural or collage of images/events important in their lives. These murals or collages can then serve as bases for small group discussions in which students expand their learning by assuming some of the teach responsibilities.

ADDITIONAL EXAMPLES

Biology

Near the end of a first-year high school biology course, the teacher schedules a discussion on the concept of biological evolution. In the teach phase the teacher divides the class into two groups—one to research the principles of evolution and the scientific evidence for it (74), and the other to research the scientific evidence for creationism. One part of the teach is to conduct the actual research that helps students prepare for the discussion. The time allotted for preparation should be significantly greater than that allotted for discussion—for example, two class periods of student preparation for each period of discussion. As another part of the teach component, the teacher should set the ground rules and objectives of the discussion. It will take two to three periods and be directed by the teacher. The objective of the discussion is to understand the scientific basis for biological evolution; consequently, only scientific evidence, pro or con, will be acceptable. Using previous learnings as evidence, students are to present their various points of view. A secondary objective as explained by the teacher, then, is for students to achieve an understanding of the nature of science and scientific knowledge (evidence).

The practice component is the discussion. The teacher initiates the discussion by simply asking, "What is evolution, and what is the scientific basis for it?" The teacher keeps the discussion on track by using a previously prepared set of questions when and if necessary. The teacher also encourages students to challenge and explore various propositions and assumptions, especially those of an emotional, supernatural, or otherwise nonscientific nature. Misinformation is similarly dealt with. Thus, the logical development of the discussion is maintained and fostered.

At the end of the discussion, the teacher has students evaluate the results by asking them the following questions:

What do we know about evolution?
What is the scientific basis for it?
Why is evolution the subject of such controversy?
Why is the controversy not *resolvable* on scientific grounds?
What were the major valid points made by each group?
What was the evidence for them?

These questions can be addressed by each student in writing or perhaps more effectively through further discussion.

In the apply component, the teacher has students reexamine the taxonomy established for the classification of living organisms established by Karl von Linné (Linnaeus) in the eighteenth century. Students are asked to support, in writing, the proposition that Linnaeus's ordering of plants and animals reflected biological evolution over a century before Darwin and Mendel initially set down its principles.

History

In a high school course in American history, the teacher decides to use a guided discussion to summarize in part the American experience as a superpower since World War II. The topic is "The Morality of Great Power Prerogatives in International Relations." By the selection of this topic the teacher has already laid the basis for a controversial interchange with at least two sides. Hence the class will naturally divide into at least two factions. As part of the teach component the teacher might logically initiate the discussion by first presenting certain great power prerogatives such as access to natural resources, dominance over markets, and establishing spheres of influence. The students should be able to identify these prerogatives and understand that they exist, based on their previous learnings about the United States and other great powers (China, France, Great Britain, the Soviet Union).

The practice phase continues with a consideration of the main question: While it may be natural for a great power to exercise these prerogatives at the expense of smaller countries, is it right? During this phase the teacher's task is to ensure that students make sound contributions by citing specific examples to support their points; to further the discussion, the teacher might ask the class to consider Jawaharlal Nehru's famous pronouncement that when elephants fight, it is the grass that suffers. In this way students can be led to the issue of competing great power prerogatives (e.g., domination of world oil supplies) and finally to the question of whether or not by their very nature international relations are actually amoral. Throughout the lesson, the teacher should encourage students to divorce themselves where possible from their "Americanness."

A product of the discussion might be to have students make summary reports applying what they have gained from the discussion specifically to the United States situation since 1945. They also might be asked to apply their new learning to similar historical circumstances such as those of nineteenth century Great Britain, especially with regard to the new United States. This can be done either in writing or perhaps, preferably, in small groups monitored by student discussion leaders.

SUMMARY

This chapter has described guided discussion in more universal terms. Like group investigations, guided discussion encourages students to inquire and to interact as a unit, as well as with the teacher. Its purposes include getting students to use and practice communication and social skills to articulate their respective points of view and to think critically as they talk with each other.

Teacher preparation is essential for the successful execution of this strategy. Teachers make at least five decisions when they plan a discussion: identifying the goals, determining the format, providing directions, determining the length of time, and deciding on the resulting product. Teachers also function as facilitators as they encourage students to examine the issues and questions and to exchange ideas. Additional skills that students learn, practice, and apply during a discussion include assuming leadership responsibilities, listening actively, and handling controversy.

Applying Your Knowledge

I. Develop a lesson using the guided discussion strategy to deal with the issue of admitting women and members of minority groups into all male organizations.

   A. What question will you develop to introduce the topic?
   B. What are your goals?
   C. What directions will you provide?
   D. What group format (small/large) will you use?
   E. What data will you present to initiate the discussion?
   F. What product will the group members have to develop?

II. Discuss cultural differences related to dress, habits, religious beliefs, human rights, and ethical behavior of public officials and business leaders.

III. For those teaching about communicating feelings and ideas through different mediums (visual, oral, written), discuss the various forms of popular advertisements and their use of color, subject, characters, as well as their roles, sex appeal, and the general market.

IV. In the vocational areas of social studies, particularly civics, develop lesson(s) using a guided discussion strategy dealing with society's responsibility to care for the elderly, the handicapped, and the indigent.

V. Discuss the different types of music that were written during times of war and peace. What themes, musical arrangements, and instruments were used?

Analysis Guide
for Guided Discussion

Did (I) the teacher—	Yes	No	N/A
1. identify a common problem?	___	___	___
2. determine a goal for the discussion?	___	___	___
3. determine the format of the group?	___	___	___
4. provide appropriate directions?	___	___	___
5. prepare a sequence of questions to elicit exchange of ideas and information?	___	___	___
6. prepare ways to deal with the verbal interaction and group dynamics?	___	___	___
7. provide for a meaningful interaction?	___	___	___
8. facilitate the expression of a variety of viewpoints?	___	___	___
9. achieve the goal of improving the speaking and thinking skills of students?	___	___	___
10. determine, define, and assign the product of the discussion?	___	___	___
11. allot enough time for the discussion?	___	___	___
12. evaluate the discussion?	___	___	___

Chapter 6
PRIMARY SOURCES
AND OTHER ARTIFACTS

DESCRIPTION

When properly analyzed and utilized, primary sources and other artifacts are evidence that allows for the possibility of reconstructing aspects of the past in the present. The ultimate goal is to gain a better understanding of both the past and the present, as well as insight into the future (37). In short, the use of these materials provides several types of knowledge. The extraction of this knowledge and/or its formulation is an intellectual activity fundamental to the teaching-learning process.

Original and/or primary sources and other artifacts are forms of evidence of the past from which knowledge is derived and on which it is based. Original (unique) and primary (closest in proximity, but not necessarily unique) sources are generally understood to include documentary evidence of peoples, civilizations, and events from the past. Similarly, artifacts are those objects that have been left behind.

The well-thought-out introduction into the classroom of artifactual material by the teacher can enhance and diversify the learning experience for secondary students in two ways—by helping them to acquire content and to develop valuable cognitive skills (28, 114). Using these materials, students can learn about the past and how to reconstruct it, accurately; also, perhaps they can gain some understanding of the real limitations of this reconstruction (2, 23, 80). As the eminent historian Carl Becker once noted, in the writing of history even the best evidence does not allow for true reconstruction of the past, but only for "shadows" of it, and in some cases the "shadows" are but mere phantoms of real shadows. For example:

Near the conclusion of a unit on the Kennedy Administration in a high school American history class, the teacher showed students a videotape compilation of various on-the-spot film records of President Kennedy's assassination so that they could see specifically what

55

happened. From these primary sources and copies of newspaper accounts that immediately followed the assassination, each student was asked to reconstruct the sequence of events in writing as fully as possible. Students then came together in small groups guided by the teacher to compare accounts. Finally, the groups were asked to list the items of controversy between the various accounts and the questions unanswered by the evidence. The class as a whole then considered the reasons for the discrepancies in the reconstructions and the unanswered questions.

To apply their knowledge and to broaden their comprehension of the content, the teacher encouraged students to reinterpret the sources by using the critical-analytical skills they were learning. By making students realize that events are not always what they seem, as well as understand the limitations of even modern film sources, the teacher helped them see something of the complexity of historical events like the Kennedy assassination and the historical continuity of which it was a part (i.e., cause and effect), and also something of the subjectivity of the historical record.

PRIMARY SOURCES AND OTHER ARTIFACTS AND TPA

The key to the fruitful use of primary sources and other artifacts and the TPA approach is planning. Careful preparation will transform "show-and-tell" into more effective teaching. The teacher provides the background of the event and puts the primary sources and artifacts into the proper perspective. Thus, in the preceding example, the students had already studied the Kennedy years, the assassination, and the official inquiries that followed. Only then were they shown the film evidence.

In the practice component, the teacher ensured the proper use of the evidence and the proper methodological (critical-analytical) approach. Individually and collectively, the students were encouraged to reconstruct the events of the assassination from the film and newspaper sources. By questioning their methods and assumptions, the teacher kept students on task. In so doing, the students were forced to consider what the films actually showed and the newspapers actually said and to separate this information from the sometimes fairly shaky interpretations they had made. In other words, they were forced back to the "hard evidence."

The use of primary sources and other artifacts is most often associated with history and social studies, but through the examples that follow, we hope to show that with advance preparation, using the TPA approach, this material can be successfully employed in other content areas as well.

ADDITIONAL EXAMPLES

Social Studies

What is a map? This activity introduces students to the complexities of maps—all that they can tell us and how they tell us. At the same time it is an experience in problem solving, viewing the map as an artifact—what a map tells us about its creators and their environment. Since maps are nonliterary documents, it also is an exercise in "graphicacy," the interpretation of data presented in graphic form.

The only resources necessary are copies of a standard state road map for each member of the class. Teachers can readily obtain these maps *free* from state highway departments. The rules are simple. During the teach, students are told that they are the leaders of an extraterrestrial "greenie" expedition that has landed on a small water planet that has a high radiation count, earth, and is orbiting a moderately sized, unimpressive yellow star. On the planet, they have found the widely scattered ruins of a long-lost civilization of which no survivors remain. All that the members of the expedition know about this civilization and its creators will be derived from the ruins and other artifacts left behind.

Road maps are the major form of evidence discovered thus far for the "leaders" to consider. Using this source, the class members who function as greenie department heads have been asked to determine what they can learn about the beings who once dominated the earth. The teacher tells students that they must play the roles of greenie scientists and technicians and that all their earthly knowledge of road maps must be forgotten. For example, once the maps are distributed, the students' first tendency will be to open them, thus showing that they are still earth people. A greenie scientist, on the other hand, would examine the folded map *in situ* first. The teacher's role, then, is to enforce this prohibition against previous earthly knowledge and to guide the analytical interchange by pointing out what kind of knowledge the greenies do possess—the state of their science and technology. Obviously, since they have journeyed far across space and time to reach the earth, the state of their science and technology is high.

The teacher continues the teach by asking questions and giving directions as needed. For example, the sequence of questions and directions might be as follows:

- What do you notice first about the artifact? (multiple copies)
- What else do you notice about it? (portable)
- And? (folded)
- Open the artifact.
- In opening it, what becomes apparent about the physiology of the being who employed it? (structural similarity)
- What else? (polychromatic vision)
- What do you notice now about the artifact? (color)
- What else do you notice about it? (line and form)
- What else? (organization)
- What types of symbols and conventions are used? (colors, letters, and numbers)
- How do you know? (scales, inset charts, directions)
- What is the artifact? (a map)
- What was it used for? (navigation on roads)
- How do you know? (how to get from place to place)
- What does the map's function tell us about its creators? (highly mobile)
- What do the material and manufacture tell us about the map's creators? (high scientific development and state of technology)
- What level of scientific and technological development is revealed by the map? (high)
- How do you know? (use of mathematics, printing, design, etc.)
- What level of aesthetic sensibility is revealed by the map? (high)
- How do you know? (use of color, line, shape, form in design)

The teacher then initiates the practice component by telling the greenie scientists-students to take the knowledge derived from the map and construct a written sketch of its creators and their civilization. They should use only information derived from and related to the map. Students will reconvene at an appointed time with their individual sketches to formulate a combined final report.

In the apply component, the greenie scientists-students are given a related artifact—a weather map copied from a local newspaper—and told to analyze it using the same rules they used for the road map.

Music

To introduce a unit on the music of the nineteenth century, a series of lessons on the romantic revolution is appropriate. As students enter the classroom, Beethoven's Third Symphony, *The Eroica*, is playing. The purpose is to sensitize them to the music they will be studying in the coming weeks. A similar technique was used during a unit on the eighteenth century when Mozart's music was the focus of study.

The teach phase continues with the teacher presenting biographical data on Beethoven and the circumstances surrounding his writing of the Third Symphony. This first major piece of romantic music by Beethoven was begun during Napoleon's rise and struggle to "liberate" Europe. Originally, it was dedicated to Napoleon, but by the time it was completed Beethoven had become disillusioned by him and his imperial dictatorship. Consequently, the dedication was changed to the German people and their war of liberation against Napoleon. Beethoven's Third Symphony is then analyzed and used to explain the nature of the romantic revolution and its art forms, especially music. In the process, the use of folk themes, specific instrumentation, and composition are pointed out and discussed.

In the practice component of the lesson, the music is replayed and students are asked to contrast and compare in writing Mozart's music with Beethoven's Third. What are the principal instruments employed in each? To what ends? Mozart and Beethoven were both Germanic, but is their music also Germanic? How was each influenced by high French culture? Through this contrast, students will gain a fuller understanding of early nineteenth century music and the revolutionary age of which it was a part.

To help students apply what they have learned, the teacher might ask them to listen to several "mystery pieces." After each selection they classify each in writing according to time period and/or historical movement based upon national themes, instrumentation, and composition. To diversify and increase the complexity of the experience, a few more modern pieces like Stravinsky's *Firebird Suite* or Copeland's *Rodeo* might be included. After listening to all the mystery pieces, students form small groups to explore their conclusions in preparation for a large group discussion. A final summary of the main points should be written on the chalkboard to bring closure to the lesson.

Mathematics

Following an introductory lesson on number systems, their arbitrary nature and historical settings, the teacher brings in several artifacts (abacuses) of ancient China for students to examine in small groups. The teacher asks students to explore the construction and workings of the abacus. How does it work? How is it used? What is it used for? When the whole class is reconvened, the teach continues with the teacher explaining how this Bronze Age calculator works, the theory behind it, and its original use.

Once they are familiar with the fundamentals of the abacus,

students are asked to practice using it individually by taking turns in solving assigned problems. As part of the practice phase, students are required to record the steps they follow in arriving at their solutions to the problems. In the process they also are told to determine the base of the number system of the abacus.

In applying this new knowledge about the abacus, students are asked to address the question: "In this age of electronic calculators, what are the advantages of using an abacus? List them in your notebooks." Should they not immediately see any advantages, the teacher can point out that a large percentage of the human race in the Soviet Union, China, and throughout Asia still uses the abacus on a daily basis. Why would so many people do so?

SUMMARY

When employing primary sources and other artifacts with the TPA approach, the major emphasis is on the teach. Students must be thoroughly prepared on the background and the method of using the evidence presented. Presentation at the appropriate time is essential. The active role of students blossoms more fully in the practice and apply components under the watchful eye of the teacher. In the process, students not only master content, but they also develop valuable critical-analytical skills as well as new insights into the nature and limitations of primary sources and other artifacts. This strategy is readily applicable to a variety of content areas; moreover, it gives students a sense of immediacy by fostering a closer attachment to the subject matter.

Applying Your Knowledge

I. Locate several issues of *Social Education* and skim the section "Document of the Month" for ideas. Develop a lesson using primary source materials housed in the National Archives. For example,

   A. Once you decide on a topic (The Home Front during the Civil War, World War I and II, Vietnam, and/or the Constitution), develop the lesson(s) that would be relevant to your curriculum.

   B. What primary source materials will you use?
      1. Letters/communiqués
      2. Films/pictures
      3. Music/art
      4.
      5.

   C. What skills do these documents emphasize?
      1. Drawing inferences
      2. Detecting biases
      3. Interpreting historic, economic, social evidence
      4.
      5.

II. Bring in copies of paintings by Grandma Moses and Clementine Hunter. Create a lesson comparing rural life in the American northeast and the Deep South, respectively, through the portrayals of these renowned folk artists.

   A. Develop the lesson(s) around the study of folk art as an expression of popular culture during various periods in American history.

   B. What primary sources will you use?
      1. Autobiography
      2. Oral tradition
      3. Crafts
      4.
      5.

   C. What skills do the sources you select emphasize?
      1. Drawing inferences
      2. Determining regional and local characteristics
      3. Understanding the life of the artist

III. Identify members of the community who participated in the American Indochina (Vietnam) experience, either as soldiers, political leaders, or in the resistance to the conflict. Have them speak to the class.

A. Develop the lesson(s) around people as primary sources.

B. What primary sources will you use?
1. Major speakers
2. Student interviews of family member participants.
3.
4.
5.

C. What skills do living sources emphasize?
1. Listening/questioning
2. Detecting biases
3. Detecting historicism
4.
5.

Analysis Guide
for Primary Sources

Did (I) the teacher—	Yes	No	N/A
1. provide the appropriate background (explain the circumstances surrounding the event/incident)?	___	___	___
2. state the purpose of using primary sources?	___	___	___
3. present steps for using primary sources?	___	___	___

Steps

	Yes	No	N/A
a. Become a witness to the event through the primary source.	___	___	___
b. Reconstruct the sequence of events based on evidence.	___	___	___
c. Interpret the purpose and intent of the material.	___	___	___
d. Be able to explain the historical, social, and economic background of the time period of the material.	___	___	___
e. Compare accounts with peers—similarities and disagreements.	___	___	___
f. Discuss questions that remain unanswered even after reading about or viewing the actual event.	___	___	___
4. emphasize that accounts may differ?	___	___	___
5. emphasize that there will be unanswered questions based on the evidence and that no source is all-inclusive?	___	___	___

Chapter 7
SIMULATIONS AND GAMING

DESCRIPTION

Pretending and simulating real-life situations are universally understood, centuries-old practices. Students are no strangers to "playing" games. In fact, many professions rely on simulations and fictitious situations to teach fundamental skills—the airline industry, for example. Participation in simulations is appropriate for students at all ages; it is an educationally sound alternative instructional strategy (84). Within a planned instructional sequence, acting out real-life situations requires students to make decisions; to use a wide range of auditory, verbal, and visual skills; and to participate in situations through character involvement. In addition, simulations and games help students deal with "problems of a very complex nature" (70). Simulations and games can be described as those "activities with goals and rules...which may...represent some other situation" and are "intended for teaching a subject or skill" (67).

Bruner (20) comments on the academic use of games:

> Games go a long way toward getting children [students] involved in understanding language, social organization, and the rest.... They provide a superb means to getting children [students] to participate actively in the process of learning—as players rather than spectators. (pp. 92–93, 95)

It should be emphasized that when considering the use of the simulation and gaming strategy, it should be "vital to...[the] total learning sequence and not...an isolated activity to be used in desperation or as a novelty" (120, p. 55).

Taylor and Walford (120) have identified three major attributes of the simulation. It is—

1. activity-oriented in which both teachers and students participate. It is a strategy used to involve students with events, people, and issues and to help them to better understand these.

64

2. problem based and interdisciplinary in nature, which involves and refines social skills.

3. dynamic, which requires flexible thinking and responsive adaptation to situations. (p. 32)

One of the major advantages of using simulations in classrooms is their ability to motivate students to participate and to heighten their interest in the situation being presented. In addition, simulations seem to be appropriate for students of differing cognitive abilities (120). Lastly, simulations provide students opportunities to communicate with others by speaking through a specific character and to receive feedback from *their* peers.

Despite all these advantages however, there are a few disadvantages. First, simulations require a great deal of class time; therefore they should be used when direct instruction or any other strategy would be less effective. Second, cost can be high, particularly if computer simulations and commercial products are used. Cost need not be a major stumbling block though— adaptations can be made to existing simulations. Third, a word of caution should be sounded: simulation activities should be implemented with great care so as not to oversimplify complex situations or events or to violate a student's integrity (8).

When designing and/or using a simulation or game, the following questions should be considered (1, 15, 47):

1. What will be the focus of the simulation?

2. What is the purpose (objective) of the simulation?

3. What are the scope and content of the simulation?

4. What student skills will be developed using the simulation?

5. What resources, materials, and equipment are required?

6. Which students will participate, and what roles will they assume in the simulation?

7. What are the rules and are they comprehensible to students and appropriate for use in school situations?

8. What steps should be taken to "run through" the simulation before involving students?

9. What questions will be asked during the discussion?

In any simulation or game, be it Sunshine, Space Flights, Star Power, World Democracy, or Smog, students are involved in several activities:

1. Assuming roles of real people who are responsible for making decisions in the situation in which they are cast
2. Experiencing the consequences of the decisions they make
3. Devising strategies as they confront risky situations
4. Analyzing the relationship that developed between their decisions and the results of those decisions
5. Working together and developing cooperative strategies.

Through these activities students are asked to make policy decisions, to declare war, to set terms for an economic summit, and so on. In addition, they begin to see how these decisions and specific situations affect human behavior. Along with these skills, students expand their vocabulary as they use terms and concepts in context. After participating in a simulation, students often have a different attitude about issues and acquire a more realistic understanding of the actual people involved (67, 87, 117).

SIMULATIONS AND GAMING AND TPA

Today much is heard about the great benefits that chemical manufacturers make available to society in eradicating disease, prolonging life, and increasing food production. Nevertheless, some people question the potential of these companies for harming the people and the communities in which they are located (e.g., Bhopal, India).

A chemistry class is focusing on the economic and social impact of chemical companies on people and society as a whole. The simulation is introduced as part of the teach, together with a brief explanation about the simulation in general, the objectives, and the roles (presidents of companies, health officials, citizens, government agents). After this explanation, groups are formed, roles are assigned, and written directions and other pertinent materials such as annual reports, court records of cases filed against the companies, and the companies' written response to the charges are distributed.

66

The practice starts when students "play" their respective roles; the teacher monitors student involvement and answers questions and moves stalled groups. But the teacher refrains from coaching students on the "right" moves and responses. A discussion following the simulation brings the practice to a close. The discussion can be considered a debriefing during which students reflect on their experiences and personal feelings (77). The discussion attempts to clarify the issues, situations, and misunderstood concepts. In addition, it gives students an opportunity to reflect on what just took place and to share how they feel. At some point in the discussion, students discuss how the simulation related to the topic of the economic and social impact of chemical companies on people and society.

When structuring the discussion, the following format may prove helpful. First, focus on the simulation/game itself, then draw some general conclusion and determine relationships between the decisions made, the strategies used, and the outcome. Finally, have students formulate the cause-and-effect relationships and make comparisons between the conditions in the simulation and the real-life situations of the Bhopal disaster.

At the end of the practice, it may be helpful to have students as part of the apply participate in the *same* simulation for a second time, since they have a better understanding of the rules, the objectives, and the relationship to a real-life situation. If the simulation is not played out a second time, students can be asked to apply the information they have acquired to the political influence of chemical companies—for example, in such areas as federal and state regulations (the dumping of chemical wastes on land and in oceans), lobbying activities, support of political candidates, the tax base, and the benefits offered by states to attract these companies.

ADDITIONAL EXAMPLES

Life Science

To review student learnings about biomes in a middle school earth science course, the teacher decides to employ a quick one-period game. A lottery is used to determine the order of play. The first student asks the first question of the others, who answer questions in turn; then the second student asks questions of the others, and so on. A right answer is worth one point; a wrong answer loses one point. The first student to get 15 points wins. The questions have been prepared by the teacher and categorized according to the biome (rain forest, desert, taiga, etc.). Students spin a wheel to select the categories, which are listed along with opportunities to "lose a turn" or "take an extra turn."

For bonus points, students are asked to analyze why an answer is wrong, given the characteristics of the specific biome. For example, for the question, "Name an animal upon which tundra nomads are dependent for their livelihood?" an appropriate answer might be caribou or yak. (Horse would be an inappropriate answer because horses would find it difficult to survive the harsh weather and feed on the tundra.) The game also can be replayed with effective results by increasing the degrees of difficulty and/or specificity of the questions and answers.

Government

To teach a high school state and local government class about local politics and the often-confusing precinct-level convention process, the teacher decides to have students play PRECON (118). The Precinct Convention Game will introduce students to their future real-life roles as voters in their state and in the United States. The total experience of the game also will provide a laboratory situation for understanding and analyzing political processes and subprocesses. Among other reasons, the teacher has carefully selected this game because it can be played by the whole class, up to thirty students, and it will take only about two hours to play. Not only is it economical of time, but its relative brevity is also intended to create pressure similar to that of a real precinct convention.

After studying the script for "Instructor" to become familiar with the game, the teacher must selectively assign roles and have students study the "Instructions for Players" and the "Game Scenario." The students are then assigned to groups according to their designated roles and the game begins with the teacher acting as monitor. Beyond the individual objectives assigned to each role, each group has the same three objectives.

1. To obtain the maximum number of group members as delegates
2. To elect convention and delegation officers
3. To pass resolutions offered by group members.

Points are awarded for the realization of individual and group objectives.

When the game is over, the teacher leads a discussion analyzing the politics and political processes encountered. To further apply what they have learned, students play the game again, but they are

68

assigned roles different from those they played the first time. Selective deviations from the rules might be tolerated to broaden students' understanding of the complexities of the precinct convention.

Mathematics

Games of trivia can be fun; those involving mathematics are no exception. Jim Kuhlmann of Corbett, Oregon, has developed a "math trivia" game, in which students review mathematical facts and concepts by asking questions. Thus, math trivia can be used during the practice phase of instruction.

The materials include game cards, a point chart, and a card holder. On one side, the cards contain questions related, for example, to the history of mathematics, computers, geometry, and measurement. On the other side of the cards are the answers. A few sample questions: "What is a bit?" "What does BASIC mean?" "What are two intersecting lines that are not perpendicular called?" Certainly the topics can be expanded and the question bank increased. Each category of topics is numbered. Teams roll the dice to determine which set of questions they will answer.

A unique feature of math trivia as developed by Kuhlmann is that it combines features of cooperative learning with a gaming strategy. For example, teams (triads) compete against each other; the team that earns 15 points first wins the game. During the apply, students could write additional questions to be added to the question bank or they could create a new set of circumstances/content and design their own game.

Other Helpful Educational Activities

Science teachers may find the series *The Search for Solutions—Teaching Notes* (published by Playback Associates for Phillips Petroleum Public Affairs) helpful. The ideas and materials can be used and copied because they are not copyrighted. Science teachers who would like to receive the printed materials as well as the videotapes can call 1–800–223–1928. A fossil finder guide and the puzzled earth activity are included for earth science teachers.

The Fossil Finder, developed by Gerald Mallmann of Somers, Wisconsin, can be used in the field in place of a cumbersome fossil guide to help identify fossils. Directions and a pattern for the fossil finder are included in the written materials mentioned above. The Fossil Finder is made of two circles fastened together to form a wheel. Students can turn the lower circle to a specific fossil, identify their find, and use the timeline to date their fossil.

The Puzzled Earth, designed by Robert Groover of Wilmington, Delaware, uses map pieces to teach the theory of continental drift (see Figure 7.1). Using the pattern provided, students are asked to unscramble the continents so that they fit together by matching mountain ranges of the same age. Students could use different colors to identify mountain ranges of different ages. After they try to fit the map pieces together, the teacher can use an overhead projector transparency to show how the pieces are matched.

Earth science teachers can use these two activities as part of gaming/activity strategies during the practice and apply phases of the lesson.

SUMMARY

Simulations and games can be valuable strategies when teachers want to recreate situations through character involvement. Students using this approach within the teach-practice-apply format are required to make decisions, to think flexibly, and to adapt to a given situation. When considering the use of a simulation or game, teachers should consider the issue/dilemma, the purpose, the scope and content, the skills to be developed, the resources, materials and equipment needed, the rules to guide the strategy, and the questions to ask when students analyze what occurred.

Students throughout time have always enjoyed simulating real-life situations. Simulations and games provide viable instructional options for replicating "real" events that students only read about in books. Thus learning can come alive by participating in the scenario as history unfolds before their eyes.

Figure 7.1

GREENLAND

350-850 MY
850-1500 MY
1550-2400 MY
2400-2900 MY

SOUTH AMERICA

2000 MY

500 MY

AFRICA

2000 MY

500 MY

350-800 MY

1550-2400 MY

2400-2900 MY

850-1550 MY

350-850 MY

1500-2400 MY

2400-2900 MY

250-350 MY

NORTH AMERICA

350-850 MY

350-850 MY

1550-2400 MY

EUROPE

250-350 MY

250-350 MY

Less than 250 MY

250-350 MY

2,000,000,000 Year Old Jigsaw

The Puzzled Earth

Applying Your Knowledge

I. You are teaching a unit on contemporary society and life in the inner city; you would like your students to have a better understanding of the cost of living, rent structure, condition of housing (apartments), city codes, and the public's inability to pay for bare essentials.

A. Identify the objectives.

B. Discuss the historical and present context of the simulation/game.

C. Develop the rule and procedures of the simulation dealing with—
  1. Income of citizens
  2. Rents and collection
  3. Payment
  4. Eviction
  5. Expenses of landlords

D. Identify characters and roles for students.

E. Develop group response sheets/tables/graphs for students to use.

F. Write and develop questions for discussion.

G. Collect materials/equipment.

II. In a government/civics class students can participate in a mock election to involve them in the campaigning process and develop the skills needed to maneuver in the political area.

III. Using science as a focus, the teacher presents the following situations:

A. Using planetary maps of the moon, Mars, and Venus (supplied by NASA), set out on an imaginary voyage of discovery and exploration of the inner planets of our solar system.

Chart your course between and on the planets (e.g., to visit "canals" on Mars). Record your trip's itinerary and progress on your ship's log (e.g., The Log of the Spirit of the Challenger).
  1. Climate

72

2. Life forms
3. Water
4. Topography
5.
6.

B. Let's pretend—How would you function if you were—
1. a green plant (e.g., broccoli)?
   a. How do you eat?
   b.
   c. How do you stand?
   d.
2. a computer?
   a. Do you think?
   b. What school did you attend?
   c. How do you store information?
   d.
3.
4.

Analysis Guide
for Simulation and Gaming

Did (I) the teacher—	Yes	No	N/A
1. structure the simulation/game so that its objectives and its relation to the topic were clearly evident?	——	——	——
2. identify roles and students for those roles?	——	——	——
3. provide written descriptions of roles for students to use initially?	——	——	——
4. have resources (materials) available to use effectively during the simulation/game?	——	——	——
5. explain the roles and objectives of the simulation/game before students began?	——	——	——
6. monitor as the simulation/game was being acted out/played?	——	——	——
7. conduct a discussion to reconstruct the sequence of events, the cause-and-effect relationships?	——	——	——
8. provide enough time?	——	——	——
9. provide closure to the simulation/game?	——	——	——
10. provide application activities following the simulation?	——	——	——

Chapter 8
COOPERATIVE LEARNING

DESCRIPTION

Cooperation is an activity in which humans work together toward an agreed-upon goal. Slavin (104, 105, 106, 107, 108) takes this concept into the classroom. He asks us to imagine a classroom in which students are working in teams rather than in the typical teacher-directed question-and-answer sessions. In the latter situation, grades and competition among students are commonplace (108, p. 7). Competition is not necessarily unhealthy, but it should be structured properly and used with those who find it a challenge. For students who continually experience failure or success, competition establishes norms that govern classroom behavior. These norms may be inaccurate for individual performance. But the "losers" can experience success when they participate in a different instructional setting.

Working together toward a common end is not new for students; teachers have used this approach with group laboratory activities, projects, and discussions. The cooperative learning described in this chapter, however, is based on two important elements that set it apart from these other instructional strategies: (1) "groups must be rewarded for doing well as a group"; and (2) "the group's success must depend on the individual learning of each group member, as when team members' quiz scores are added together to form a total team score" (107, p. 8).

Students who participate in cooperative learning groups develop a sense of esprit de corps; their attitude is that group members are important and are rooting for each other. Also, "doing your own work" is not an integral part of this strategy. In these groups students begin to demand excellence from each other, in terms of explaining concepts and skills, helping one another while discussing what is to be learned, and high quiz scores.

According to Slavin (108), cooperative learning is an instructional strategy "in which students of all performance levels work together in small groups toward a common goal" (p. 8). This chapter presents this strategy in the light of several group approaches that have developed in the last fifteen years. From all the findings, the news about these programs is positive.

Research on cooperative learning (107) has been collected at various grade levels (2–12), from diverse school systems (rural, suburban, and urban), and in numerous curriculum areas (mathematics, social studies, science, and language arts). Student achievement in these studies was measured by standardized tests; in thirty out of thirty-five studies of cooperative classes, student achievement was high (107).

According to these and other studies, better results occur with cooperation than with intense competition. In a competitive classroom, only a few students can be number one and winners. What happens to the other students? Cooperative learning is equally beneficial to all; as a result, all students learn. In fact, they learn, practice, and apply more skills than meet the eye. A positive work ethic, working productively with others, an increased degree of retention, and problem-solving abilities are only a few of the by-products of team learning. The old adage that two heads are better than one is the crux of the strategy.

Several approaches can be included in cooperative learning. One is the Student Teams Achievement Divisions (STAD) developed at Johns Hopkins University (101). A teacher who uses STAD introduces new concepts each week by lecture or discussion. After this introduction, students organized in teams of four or five members are responsible for mastering the new material by completing worksheets, working problems, and explaining concepts to each other. The only individual activity is to take the quiz, but the scores are reported as a team score. The emphasis of STAD is to improve; there is no automatic "strikeout"— everyone is successful (108). For more specific information, see the Bibliography for a listing of articles and monographs by Slavin. According to a recent study conducted in a low-achieving high school math class, students who participated in STAD "scored more than 50 percent higher than the control classes on a math test" (107, p. 9).

To demonstrate individual mastery of ideas and skills, students might play weekly games as part of a tournament rather than taking a quiz. Teams-Games-Tournament (TGT) developed by David De Vries and Keith Edwards is organized around students who demonstrate their knowledge by competing with other students of comparable ability to add points to the team score. Although the tournament tables change every week, the teams remain intact for at least a six-week period.

Another member of the cooperative learning family is Team Assisted Individualization (TAI) (109). TAI combines cooperative learning and individually paced instruction. This strategy assigns students to teams comprised of four or five heterogeneous members. Team membership is based on the results of a diagnostic test. Once team assignments are made, each student is given a self-paced program. Within the team pairs of students work together exchanging ideas, checking answers on assignment sheets, etc. Before taking the quiz individually, each student must pass the "checkout" with a score of 80 percent or better. By the end of the week, all student test scores become a part of the team's score. The use of TAI is ideal for classes that are too diverse to use the same materials at the same time. For example, TAI students in a study "gained 1.63 grade equivalents in mathematics computations in eighteen weeks, while control students gained only .61 grade equivalents" (107, p. 9).

Other members of the cooperative learning family that secondary teachers may wish to explore are Jigsaw (5), Learning Together (59), and group investigation (98).

Cooperation is not always a skill that students understand or can easily put into practice. Often, teachers need to be direct and teach the skills necessary to participate in cooperative learning teams. According to Johnson and Johnson (60), "Good group members are made, not born." These researchers have outlined five helpful steps for teaching cooperation (110):

1. Helping students understand that in relation to learning subject area concepts, skills, and information, "none of us is as smart as all of us."
2. Decide on the individual skills and/or concepts to be learned and be sure they are clearly understood.
3. Provide students with simulations in which they can practice these concepts and skills.
4. Provide individual students feedback regarding their cooperative behavior in team settings.
5. Have students practice the concepts and skills.

COOPERATIVE LEARNING AND TPA

When using cooperative learning with TPA, the teach includes identifying the content and/or skills to be learned, providing the basic introductory and other information necessary to allow the groups to function, and organizing the student groups. For example:

In an earth science course unit on pollution, the teacher begins the teach with remarks about the location of industrial and/or nuclear energy plants, airports, major highways, and waste disposal sites. As necessary as they are, power sources, transportation, and industry are responsible for producing harmful by-products such as noise, toxic waste, radiation, smog, and other forms of pollution. As part of the cooperative learning strategy, students are asked to make decisions about allowing the location of a nuclear power plant in their community. A basic fact to be considered—a coal-burning plant is already in operation about 300 miles to the south.

To aid in making an intelligent decision, during the practice several laboratory and nonlaboratory activities will be carried out. One group of students will calculate the radiation levels for specific cities, including their own. (See Figure 8.1.) A second group will determine the acidity of common substances such as grass, rocks, leaves, and water. (See Figure 8.2.) And a third group will study water quality by testing samples for lead, cyanide, PCB, and other pollutants. Each group will compile and file an "official" report; the group with the most convincing argument for or against locating a nuclear power plant in the area, based on the data collected, will receive the total 50 points.

During the apply component, the findings of each group will be shared with the class to determine the positive and negative ramifications on the community of the construction of a nuclear power plant. Each group will then prepare a final impact statement. As part of the application phase, a class election will be held. All students will be asked to vote yea or nay on this issue and to explain their positions in light of their group report and the final impact statement. Descriptions of group activities one and two can be found in Figures 8.1 and 8.2.

FIGURE 8.I
Calculating Annual Totals and Radiation*
(in millirems)

The amount of cosmic radiation that reaches earth is *44*. Add 1 for every 100 feet above sea level because cosmic radiation is changed by the atmosphere.

Pittsburgh is 1200 ft.	+12
Denver is 5300 ft.	+53
Atlanta is 1050 ft.	+10
Chicago is 600 ft.	+ 6
Coastal cities are at sea level, so	+ 0
If a house is made of brick or concrete	+45
stone	+50
wood	+35
The average ground radiation is	15
The average water, food, air radiation is	25
Nuclear weapons testing fallout is	4
Chest X ray	+ 9
Flying—for each I500 flying miles	+ 1
Intestinal X rays	+210
5-mile radius of a coal-fired power plant	+0.3
TOTAL:	

*Adapted from the Volunteer Action People Publication, P.O. Box 355, Pittsburgh, PA I5230, presented in *The Search for Solutions: Teaching Notes.*

FIGURE 8.2
Acid Rain: What Is Normal?*

Ask students to collect a variety of materials—for example, soil, leaves, decaying matter, grass, rocks, and water. The soil samples should come from different places in the community. The location of each find should be recorded. Take each sample and grind and mix it with distilled water. Then, use litmus paper to test each solution to determine if it is acidic or alkaline. To take it a step further, use an indicator (available at most nurseries) to determine the degree of acidity or alkalinity. Test each sample solution over a period of time, perhaps after several days, and record the findings on a pH scale.

What substances are acid? What substances are alkaline? Are more substances acidic or alkaline? What is the most acidic substance? Most alkaline? What role does location play?

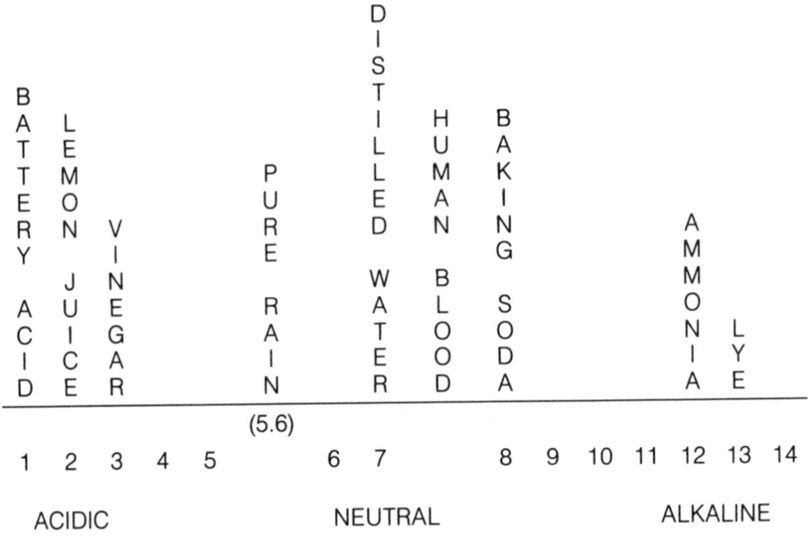

```
                              D
                              I
                              S
        B                     T
        A   L             H   B
        T   E             U   A
        T   M         P   L   K
        E   O         U   L   I
        R   N  V      R   E   N              A
        Y   |  |      E   D   G              M
            J  N          W   B              M
        A   U  E      R   A   L   S          O
        C   I  G      A   T   O   O       L
        I   C  A      I   E   O   D   N   Y
        D   E  R      N   R   D   A   I   E
                                         A
    _____
                (5.6)
     1   2   3   4   5      6   7      8   9  10  11  12  13  14

        ACIDIC              NEUTRAL              ALKALINE
```

*Adapted from The Spark, Duke Power Company, Charlotte, NC, presented in *The Search for Solutions: Teaching Notes.*

ADDITIONAL EXAMPLES

Foreign Language

At the outset of a first-year foreign language class—for example, Russian—the teacher organizes students into groups to write simple one-act plays to be presented at the "Grand Festival of Russian Drama" at the end of the first semester. The plays are to demonstrate the students' mastery of written and spoken Russian for the first half of the school year. To further demonstrate their mastery, while one group is performing its final product, the other groups will be assisting the teacher in judging the performance by completing specially prepared rating sheets. Points will be awarded to each group based on the quality of individual performances—pronunciation, accent, expression, accuracy of word usage, and authenticity of time period. The total quality of the written text (Cyrillic alphabet, vocabulary, and grammar used) will be rated as well. In the teach component, the teacher not only establishes the ground rules for the cooperative activity, leading to the eventual competition and judging, but also carries out the language instruction over the course of four months. During the teach, various activities compatible with cooperative learning are employed. The teacher also must be available to consult with individual groups and guide them in the creation of their production.

The students practice in groups what they are learning through various assignments and exercises, including quizzes and tests, which are completed individually. As part of cooperative learning, group members earn points for the team as a whole. The drama festival with its performances, competition, and judging becomes the apply component of TPA. Remember that costumes, staging, plot, etc., all count as part of the final scoring of the festival production, and that appropriate certificates, medals, and/or trophies based on point totals received should be awarded to all members of a group and to all groups.

In much the same way a presummer vacation grand festival could be organized for the second half of the school year. If the teacher chose to use the one-act productions after one semester, perhaps a larger, two-act play should be the objective for the end of the year. The group compositions could change or remain intact. However, if the teacher decided on only one festival—to take place at the end of the year—the suggestions for the one-act play should be used. In addition, since all previous ratings are made public, groups can assess strengths as well as weaknesses.

Social Studies

What is a revolution? To introduce a unit on this topic, the teacher initiates a discussion on the nature and causes of political revolutions in the modern world to determine if such occurrences have any common denominators. Drawing on their previous knowledge of specific revolutions and the term "revolution" in general, the students, guided by the teacher, eventually settle on five basic aspects common to most revolutions:

I. Leadership
2. Unifying Ideology
3. Popular support (at least the neutrality of the people)
4. Significant source of distress (oppression)
5. Weak target (prospect for success).

Although each of these elements may vary in importance according to the specific revolution under consideration, all five must be present for a revolution to have a chance to succeed.

The teacher then groups the students, assigning each group a specific major revolution—American, Chinese, French, Indian, Mexican, and Russian—to investigate. Each group member is assigned one of the five basic aspects listed. Each member is then responsible for teaching the group about his/her aspect and its role in the group's revolution. All students will be required to take individual tests related to the topic of revolution and to the examples they are studying in their groups. Test scores will be recorded as team scores.

Group members then practice what they have learned cooperatively by formulating and writing a group report on their specific revolution, emphasizing which of the five aspects are of greater consequence and which of lesser consequence. The teacher evaluates each group's report and assigns it a score (made up of the scores of individual members for their contributions to the report), which is to be added to the group's previous totals.

Individually and collectively, the students in their groups apply what they have learned from their revolution by evaluating the other revolutions in writing, based on the other group reports. This is essentially a "compare and contrast" exercise to broaden understanding of the concept of revolution and to validate the original hypothesis of the five common denominators. In this activity each group teaches the others about its revolution and learns from and has an opportunity to critique the conclusions of other groups. Individual group members' evaluations receive a score and are totaled with the group's previous scores to determine final group scores and standings.

This approach also works well with other general themes—such as the role of barbarians (Germans, Mongols, Turks, etc.) in the development of civilizations, and eras of transition (Hellenistic Civilization, Renaissance, post-World War II years, etc.—as long as the teacher carefully develops and explains a working hypothesis to be followed and tested by students.

SUMMARY

Students succeed as members of a group. Team members encourage each other to work together and to excel for the good of the whole. Students working in pairs within a team gain greater self-esteem, like school more, develop norms that provide an incentive to do their best, feel in control of their own learning, and remain on task for longer periods of time.

Positive student outcomes are not always found in all research findings; this is not the case, however, with cooperative learning research. There is evidence to prove that all students can and do benefit not only socially but academically from learning cooperatively. Based on several studies at both the elementary and secondary levels, the research data indicate that cooperative learning contributes to improved student achievement, to a better understanding of the material among team members, and to increased concern for others. The degree of change in student behaviors depends on the way the cooperative groups work together; simply allowing students to complete activity sheets in small groups, for example, is not in the spirit of cooperative learning (104, p. 657).

One of the pluses for the use of this strategy is its inexpensiveness. Teachers do not need costly equipment or supplies to implement cooperative learning; nor do they need to spend extensive time in preparing special instructional materials. Rather, the materials they normally use in their classes can be organized and sequenced in a different way. Finally, the most significant change is that of student attitude—a result that makes the idea of teamwork truly valuable.

Applying Your Knowledge

I. Using information from various forms of current media, discern and investigate the major issues confronting the United States and the Soviet Union in order to understand the current state of American-Soviet relations.

A. Media sources
   I. Newspapers
   2. Newsmagazines
   3. Videotapes
   4.
   5.

B. Issues identified and assigned to groups
   I. Arms control
   2. Cultural relations
   3. Central America
   4. China
   5.
   6.
   7.

C. Evaluation system
   I. General group reports
      a. Oral presentations
      b. Written summaries
         (I) By presenting group
         (2) By students in audience
   2. More specific individual papers
   3. Other audience response
   4.
   5.

D. Product
   I. Use a visual (flow chart) constructed from parts from all groups to document the current state of American-Soviet relations.
   2.
   3.

II. By having students in their groups study examples of works from various late nineteenth and early twentieth century artistic movements, formulate as a class the foundations of modern art.

A. Examples
   1. Painting
   2. Sculpture
   3. Film
   4.
   5.

B. Movements identified and assigned to groups
   1. Impressionism
   2. Futurism
   3. Surrealism
   4.
   5.
   6.

C. Evaluation system
   1. Group presentations
      a.
      b.
   2. Specific individual written reports
   3.
   4.
   5.

D. Product
   1. Syntheses of foundations
      a.
      b.
   2.

Analysis Guide
for Cooperative Learning

Did (I) the teacher—	Yes	No	N/A
I. organize groups that are compatible and productive?	___	___	___
2. have a common goal for students to work toward?	___	___	___
3. establish an evaluation system in which individual work is rewarded as part of the total group effort?	___	___	___
4. have quizzes developed for individuals to take?	___	___	___
5. structure and sequence activities that ensure that students are teaching each other?	___	___	___
6. help students understand the idea that "none of us is as smart as all of us"?	___	___	___
7. provide feedback during each component of TPA?	___	___	___

Chapter 9
PUTTING IT ALL TOGETHER

INTRODUCTION

The first eight chapters of this text identified teaching strategies that impact on student learning. Although the use of any of these instructional strategies does not necessarily make the teacher's job easier, through a desire to vary and improve instruction, "teachers can become more productive...[with] a sense of direction and purpose" (17, p. 3). In their quest for professional growth, then, secondary teachers may use different strategies to achieve specific learning goals.

To use instructional strategies effectively, secondary teachers must make the key decisions to foster change. For Lovell and Wiles (68), "instructional improvement implies change..." (p. 114). Clearly, making decisions is an integral part of directing the change process; and our assumption is that there is always room for improvement and growth no matter how effective or successful a teacher may be.

According to Joyce, Showers, and Rolheiser-Bennett (63), there are four promising practices for student learning and professional growth: (1) instructional strategies, (2) curriculum organization and implementation, (3) effective teaching, and (4) effective schools. This text has concentrated on instructional strategies using the conceptual framework of teach-practice-apply and effective teaching behaviors. The TPA framework is not meant to be a strict formula that squeezes the vitality out of teaching; on the contrary, teach, practice, and apply are essential components of every lesson. TPA offers secondary teachers another way to view teaching as they make decisions about their instructional behavior.

Varying instructional strategies can be considered innovative, but it is equally important that teachers require students to practice what has been taught and to apply that information beyond a specific context or situation. Research suggests that student learning increases when teachers select particular strategies to achieve specific outcomes such as learning concepts, developing discussion and analytical skills, and so on. For example, the research "on cooperative learning is overwhelmingly positive, and the cooperative approaches are appropriate for all curriculum areas" (63).

This text has described a variety of teaching strategies within the TPA format to bring about behavioral instructional changes and at the same time to increase student involvement in the learning process. As Sizer (100) points out, students should "get into the habit of figuring things out for themselves" (p. 15). Encouraging students to think improves the educational practices within individual classrooms and schools. Encouraging teachers to grow professionally and students to think critically are among the primary objectives of education.

By presenting several instructional strategies within the context of TPA, we have attempted to expand each teacher's knowledge base by suggesting that curricular information can be handled at higher levels of Bloom's taxonomy. As Sizer observes, "rushing to get past the Bill of Rights so we can reach Grover Cleveland by Valentine's Day" (100, p. 15) is not a legitimate goal of education. It is imperative that adolescent learning be taken seriously; this implies attempting and using new ways of teaching.

It also is naive to assume that teachers stop learning when they earn their teaching credentials. Therefore, teachers, not necessarily supervisors, should determine what this learning will be. If teachers themselves do not take charge of the change process, another person or agency will do so. This chapter suggests ways that secondary teachers can "put it all together"—by using self-evaluation and making professional decisions. We agree with Sergiovani and Starratt's (96) description of the function of professional development as "more a function of the teacher's changing as a person—of seeing himself or herself, the school, the curriculum and students differently" (p. 327). How does change take place, then, and how can teachers facilitate it in their own instructional behavior?

FACILITATING CHANGE

According to Frymier (38), "in any attempt to improve education, teachers are central" (p. 9). This centrality means empowering teachers to make decisions and to teach effectively. To be effective, teachers must focus on their teaching and evaluate their strengths and weaknesses. After reading this text, secondary teachers should reflect on the types of strategies they would like to use as they teach their respective subjects. First, though, it is our belief that to be truly effective, teachers should have a keen sense of what they do best, and be in control of what they learn. Once they have an understanding of who they are, they are ready to make decisions about what they need to do to improve.

Indeed, this sense of self is the key to professional growth and development. In the light of what is known about effective teaching, along with the information presented about specific instructional strategies within the TPA format, self-evaluation can help teachers as they strive for excellence. Bruner (19) believes that "unless the learner [teacher] also masters himself, disciplines his taste, deepens his view of the world, the 'something' [obtained]...is hardly worth the effort of transmission" (p. 73). The Appendix describes several instruments that will help teachers as they engage in the self-evaluation process (82, pp. 57–59).

Making changes requires making decisions. Gorton (48) identifies seven steps in the decision-making process:

Step I. Define the situation.
Step 2. Identify the alternatives.
Step 3. Assess the alternatives.
Step 4. Select the best possible alternative.
Step 5. Secure acceptance of the decision.
Step 6. Implement the decision.
Step 7. Evaluate the decision. (p. 6)

Like Gorton, we view decision making as problem solving that can lead to positive instructional changes in the teacher's classroom behavior.

Other methods to help increase instructional excellence and facilitate improvement in delivering instruction are peer coaching and videotaping. In "The Coaching of Teaching," Joyce and Showers (61) place the responsibility for change on teachers themselves. These authors suggest taking four steps to successfully implement any change in instructional behavior. The four steps constitute the "coaching" process:

1. Studying the rationale and description of the teaching strategy.
2. Observing a teacher who effectively uses the strategy.
3. Practicing and receiving technical feedback from peers in a protected environment away from students.
4. Coaching group members as they integrate the strategy into their teaching repertoire and teaching area.

"Coaching," then, involves not only peer feedback on the appropriate use of certain strategies when teaching specific concepts, but also professional support and encouragement so that teachers use these strategies regularly and effectively. Coaching teams allow teachers to develop the appropriate instructional skills and to transfer them to "real" classroom situations. These training sessions continue after several practices. Only after mastering the instructional strategy and using it in specific teaching situations with different student populations can a teacher be said to have implemented the strategy successfully. Most importantly, coaching encourages teachers to become true colleagues—companions and team members who share and learn from each other.

Through such collegial activities, positive and permanent change in the pursuit of instructional excellence is possible. Coaching is a means of helping teachers learn "how to *become* good teachers" (124, p. 4). For good teaching to occur, three essential conditions should be met: autonomy, collaboration, and time (124). Teachers who are truly interested in improvement need to have the freedom to direct what and how they learn. "The key to teacher satisfaction and learning . . . is teacher ownership of the process" (40, p. 25). Whether experienced or new, teachers in this type of school environment are encouraged to experiment and try new strategies. Individual experimentation, a trait of successful businesses, stressed by Peters and Waterman (*In Search of Excellence: Lessons from America's Best-Run Companies* [Harper-Row, 1982]), is also applicable to schools. Freedom coupled with collaboration results in a work environment that loosens the grip of professional isolation. For such interaction to occur, time is necessary. But the time teachers spend learning how to use a new strategy is time well spent. Self-evaluation, along with coaching, helps teachers determine what changes they need to make or what strategies will work for them, while they are simultaneously in touch with other professionals.

The cornerstones of making changes are technology and collaboration. The use of videotaping and working in small groups with peers can help teachers "transfer knowledge of instructional skills into active classroom practice" (89, p. 64). First, the camera captures on tape an unalterable picture of each strategy practiced and its application to specific concepts and topics. Then, the taped lesson becomes the focus of discussion as peer group members analyze the tape and offer the teacher corrective feedback. As teachers take turns being videotaped, they coach each other in the successful use and implementation of each strategy against the backdrop of the TPA paradigm.

One teacher's comments provide an apt description of the process: "I can see what happened, not what I thought had happened . . . Self-evaluation is most valuable to me" (89, p. 67). The use of videotaping helps to build "communities of teachers who continuously engage in the study of their craft" (99). Peer coaching coupled with videotaping permits "teachers to direct and manage their own professional growth" because they can see themselves and benefit from comments made by peers (89, p. 67).

SUMMARY

This chapter has provided specific methods that secondary teacher can use to initiate and realize change. Because change takes time and is dislocating, support from colleagues can make the process more rewarding and long lasting.

This book has provided the first step for facilitating change by offering an alternative model for instructional diversity in secondary classrooms. The acid test for the ideas presented for instructional strategies and the conceptual framework of teach, practice, and apply will take place when teachers use these strategies in their classrooms and make permanent changes in their teaching repertoire. The role of the teacher in the change process is one that gives force, direction, and personal meaning to what takes place in the classroom. Changes are accomplished by and through people and are personal experiences (53). As Fullan notes (39), "any significant innovation, if it is to result in change, requires individual implementers to work out their own meaning" (p. 40).

We believe teachers can and must develop a mindset for change. Some of the key reasons for avoiding and/or resisting change are a lack of understanding, a lack of skill, and an element of uncertainty. Our goal has been to help facilitate the change process by presenting research data on effective teaching, individual teaching strategies, and the TPA paradigm, and then translating these into workable educational practices that can easily be accepted and implemented into classroom life.

We feel that the TPA model, in combination with the recommendations for implementing alternative strategies, will enable secondary teachers not only to make the long-term beneficial changes mandated by their critics, but also to make their instruction more creative and meaningful.

Appendix
TEACHER SELF-ASSESSMENT INSTRUMENTS

PHILOSOPHICAL BELIEF SYSTEM

The Scale of Cognitive Structures is a questionnaire designed to identify an individual's philosophical orientation. Items are keyed to represent three dominant philosophical strains in American culture: traditionalism, pragmatism/progressivism, and existentialism. The instrument and manual may be obtained from

Scale of Cognitive Structures
O.P. Esteves
College of Education
Texas Tech University
Lubbock, TX 79409

INTERPERSONAL AWARENESS TRAITS

The Fundamental Interpersonal Relations Orientation-Behavior (FIRO-B) is designed to measure an individual's characteristic behavior toward others in the areas of inclusion, control, and affection. This instrument is also designed to stress relationships between people, such as compatibility or coefficiency. It may be obtained from

Fundamental Interpersonal Relations Orientation-Behavior (FIRO-B)
William C. Schutz
Consulting Psychological Press
577 College Avenue
Palo Alto, CA 94306

From *Improving Middle School Instruction: A Research-Based Self-Assessment System* by Judy Reinhartz and Don M. Beach (Washington, D.C.: National Education Association, 1983).

SELF-CONCEPT

The Tennessee Self-Concept Scale is self-scoring and is composed of 100 self-descriptive statements, which the teacher uses to develop a picture of him/herself. The scale provides a profile that shows comparative data concerning physical self, moral-ethical self, personal self, family self, social self, identity—what he or she is, self-satisfaction—how he or she accepts him/herself, and behavior—how he or she acts. The instrument may be obtained from

Tennessee Self-Concept Scale
William H. Fritts
Counselor Recordings and Tests
Box 6184, Acklen Station
Nashville, TN 37212

LEARNING STYLE

The Productivity Environmental Preference Survey (PEPS) assesses the individual adult's personal preferences for each of 21 different elements in four major areas. This survey identifies how adults prefer to function, learn, concentrate, and perform in their occupational or educational activities in the following areas: immediate environment (sound, temperature, light, and design); emotionality (motivation, responsibility, persistence, and need for either structure or flexibility); sociological needs (self-oriented, colleague-oriented, authority-oriented, and/or combined ways); and physical needs (perceptual preference(s), time of day, intake, and mobility). The instrument may be obtained from

Productivity Environmental Preference Survey
Gary Price, Rita Dunn, and Kenneth Dunn
Price Systems, Inc.
Box 3067
Lawrence, KS 66044

Another instrument for diagnosing learning style is the Learning Style Inventory (LSI), a nine-item self-description questionnaire. Each item asks respondents to order four words in a way that best describes his or her learning style. The LSI measures an individual's relative emphasis on four learning abilities: concrete experience (CE), reflective observation (RO), abstract conceptualization (AC), and active experimentation (AE), plus two combination scores that indicate the extent to which an individual emphasizes abstractness over concreteness (AC-CE) and action over reflection (AE-RO). The instrument may be obtained from

Learning Style Inventory
David A. Kolb
McBer and Company
137 Newbury Street
Boston, MA 02116

TEACHING STYLE

The Teaching Style Inventory (TSI) provides a profile with nine major elements comprising an individual's teaching style: instructional planning, teaching methods, student groupings, room design, teaching environment, evaluation techniques, educational philosophy, teaching characteristics, and student preference. The instrument may be obtained from

Teaching Style Inventory
Rita and Kenneth Dunn
Learning Styles Network
School of Education and Human Services
St. John's University
Jamaica, NY 11439

PSYCHOLOGICAL CONSTRUCTS

The Tuckman Teacher Feedback Form (TTFF) describes the teacher as a structurer, the teacher as a problem solver, and four ways that teachers can deal with problems of control, interpersonal relations, and ambiguity. This instrument is composed of 28 paired adjectives, each pair representing a personal construct that can be used to construe the teacher's behavior. It may be obtained from

Tuckman Teacher Feedback Form
Bruce W. Tuckman
School of Education
Bernard Baruch College—CUNY
17 Lexington Avenue
New York, NY 10010

BIBLIOGRAPHY

1. Abt, C. *Final Report on the Virgin Islands Game.* Cambridge, Mass.: Abt Associates, 1966.

2. Alleman-Brooks, J.; Clegg, A.; and Sebolt, A. P. "Making the Past Come Alive." *Social Studies* 68 (January-February, 1977): 3–6.

3. Allington, R. "The Reading Instruction Provided Readers of Differing Reading Ability." *Elementary School Journal* 83 (1983): 548–59.

4. Anderson, L. M.; Evertson, C. M.; and Brophy, J. E. "An Experimental Study of Effective Teaching in First-Grade Reading Groups." *Elementary School Journal* 79 (1979): 193–222.

5. Aronson, E. *The Jigsaw Classroom.* Beverly Hills, Calif: Sage Publications, 1978.

6. Ausubel, D. *Educational Psychology: A Cognitive View.* New York: Holt, Rinehart and Winston, 1968.

7. _____. *The Psychology of Meaningful Verbal Learning.* New York: Grune and Stratton, 1963.

8. Banks, J. A. *Teaching Strategies for the Social Studies: Inquiry, Valuing, and Decision-Making.* 2d. ed. Reading, Mass.: Addison-Wesley Publishing Co., 1977.

9. Barell, J. "You Ask the Wrong Questions." *Educational Leadership* 42 (1985): 18–23.

10. Barnes, S. *Synthesis of Selected Research on Teaching Findings.* Austin, Tex.: Research and Development Center for Teacher Education, 1981.

11. Barron, R. F. "The Use of Vocabulary as an Advance Organizer." In *Research in Reading in the Content Areas: First-Year Report,* edited by H. L. Herber and P. L. Sanders. Syracuse, N.Y.: Syracuse University Reading and Language Arts Center, 1969.

12. Beez, W. *Influence of Biased Psychological Reports on Teacher Behavior and Pupil Performance.* Proceedings of the 76th Annual Convention of the American Psychological Association, 1968, pp. 605–6.

13. Bennett, W. J. *What Works: Research About Teaching and Learning.* Washington, D.C.: Department of Education, Information Office, 1986.

14. Berliner, D. "The Half-Full Glass: A Review of Research on Teaching." In *Using What We Know About Teaching,* edited by P. L. Hosford. Alexandria, Va.: Association for Supervision and Curriculum Development, 1984.

15. Boocock, S., and Schild, E. O., eds. *Simulation Games in Learning.* New York: Sage Publications, 1968.

16. Boszik, B. "A Study of Teacher Questioning and Student Response Interaction During Pre-Story and Post-Story Portions of Reading Comprehension Lessons." Paper presented at the annual meeting of the American Educational Research Association, New York City, 1982.

17. Brandt, R. "Overview: Teaching Must Be More Productive—and It Can Be." *Educational Leadership* 45 (1987): 2, 3.

18. Bruner, J. *The Process of Education.* Cambridge, Mass.: Harvard University Press, 1960.

19. _____. *Towards a Theory of Instruction.* New York: Norton, 1966.

20. Bruner, J., et al. *A Study of Thinking.* New York: John Wiley, 1967.

21. Chaikin, A.; Sigler, E.; and Derlega, V. "Nonverbal Mediators of Teacher Expectation Effects." *Journal of Personality and Social Psychology* 30 (1974): 144–49.

22. Coker, H.; Lorentz, C. W; and Coker, J. "Teacher Behavior and Student Outcomes in Georgia Study." Paper presented at the annual meeting of the American Educational Research Association, Boston, 1980.

23. Conzen, M. P. *Using Maps as Evidence: Lessons in American Social Economic History.* ERIC Document Reproduction Service, 1975. ED 125 935.

24. Cooper, H., and Baron, R. "Academic Expectations and Attributed Responsibility as Predictors of Professional Teachers' Reinforcement Behavior." *Journal of Educational Psychology* 69 (1977): 409–18.

25. Cooper, J. D., et al. *The What and How of Reading Instruction.* Columbus, Ohio: Charles E. Merrill Publishing Co., 1979.

26. Darling-Hammond, L. *Beyond the Commission Reports: The Coming Crisis in Teaching.* Santa Monica, Calif.: Rand Corp., 1984.

27. Dewey, J. *Democracy and Education: An Introduction to the Philosophy of Education.* New York: Free Press, 1966.

28. Downey, M. T. "Teaching the History of Childhood." *Social Education* 50 (April/May 1986): 4, 262–67.

29. Duffy, G., and McIntryre, L. "A Naturalistic Study of Instructional Assistance in Primary Grade Reading." *Elementary School Journal* 83 (1982): 14–23.

30. Eisner, E. W. "The Art and Craft of Teaching." *Educational Leadership* 40 (1983): 4–13.

31. Ellson, D. "Improving Productivity in Teaching." *Phi Delta Kappan* 62 (October 1986): 111–24.

32. Emmer, E.; Evertson, C.; Sanford J.; Clements, B.; and Worsham, M. *Organizing and Managing the Junior High Classroom.* Report No. 6151, Research and Development Center for Teacher Education, University of Texas at Austin, 1982.

33. Evertson, C. M.; Anderson, C.; Anderson, L.; and Brophy, J. E. "Relationship Between Classroom Behaviors and Student Outcomes in Junior High Mathematics and English Classes." *American Educational Research Journal* 17 (1980): 43–60.

34. Everston, C. M.; Emmer, E; and Brophy, J. "Predictors of Effective Teaching in Junior High Mathematics Class." *Journal of Research in Mathematics Education* 11 (1980): 167–78.

35. Fisher, C. W.; Berliner, D. C.; Tilby, N. N.; Marliave, R.; Cahen, L. S.; and Dishaw, M. M. "Teaching Behaviors, Academic Learning Time, and Student Achievement: An Overview." In *Time to Learn,* edited by C. Denham and A. Lieberman. Washington, D.C.: Department of Education, 1980.

36. Fitzpatrick, K. A. "An Investigation of Secondary Classroom Material Strategies for Increasing Student Academic Engaged Time." Unpublished doctoral dissertation, University of Illinois at Urbana-Champaign, 1981.

37. Freeman, E. T.; Bodle, W.; and Burroughs, W. "Eleanor Roosevelt Resigns from the DAR: A Study in Conscience." *Social Education,* Document of the month 48 (November/December 1984): 536–41.

38. Frymier, J. "Bureaucracy and the Neutering of Teachers." *Phi Delta Kappan* 69 (September 1987): 9–14.

39. Fullan, M. *The Meaning of Educational Change.* New York: Teachers College Press, Columbia University, 1982.

40. Garmston, R. J. "How Administrators Support Peer Coaching." *Educational Leadership* 44 (February 1987): 18–26.

41. Good, T.; Biddle, B; and Brophy, J. *Teachers Make a Difference.* New York: Holt, Rinehart and Winston, 1975.

42. Good, T., and Brophy, J. *Looking in Classrooms.* New York: Harper and Row, 1984.

43. Good, T.; Cooper, H.; and Blakey, S. "Classroom Interaction as a Function of Teacher Expectations, Student Sex, and Time of Year." *Journal of Educational Psychology* 72 (1980); 378–85.

44. Good, T. L., and Grouws, D. A. "The Missouri Mathematics Effectiveness Project." *Journal of Educational Psychology* 71 (1979): 355–62.

45. Good, T.; Grouws, D.; and Ebmeier, H. *Active Mathematics Teaching: Empirical Research in Elementary and Secondary Classrooms.* New York: Longman, 1983.

46. Goodlad, J. *A Place Called School.* New York: McGraw-Hill, 1984.

47. Gordon, A. K. *Educational Games Extension Service, Units 1–8.* Chicago: Science Research Associates, 1968.

48. Gorton, R. A. *School Leadership and Administration.* Dubuque, Iowa: William C. Brown Publishers, 1987.

49. Griffin, Gary A. "Teacher Induction: Research Issues." *Journal of Teacher Education* 36 (January/February 1985).

50. Heapy, N., and Siess, T. "Behavioral Consequences of Impression Formation: Effects of Teachers' Impressions upon Essay Evaluations." Paper presented at the annual meeting of the Eastern Psychological Association, 1970.

51. Heitzmann, W. R. *Educational Games and Simulations.* Rev. ed. Washington, D.C.: National Education Association, 1987.

52. Hoover, K. H., and Hollingsworth, P. M. *A Handbook for Elementary School Teachers.* Abridged 2d ed. Boston: Allyn and Bacon, 1978.

53. Hord, S. M., et al. *Taking Charge of Change.* Alexandria, Va: Association for Supervision and Curriculum Development, 1987.

54. Hunter, M., and Russell, D. "Planning for Effective Instruction: Lesson Design." In *Increasing Your Teaching Effectiveness.* Palo Alto, Calif.: Learning Institute, 1981.

55. Imig, D. G. "Renewal and Purpose." *AACTE* Brief 5 (March 1984): 2.

56. Jackson, P. *Life in Classrooms.* New York: Holt, Rinehart and Winston, 1968.

57. Jacobsen, D.; Eggen, P.; Kauchak, D.; and Dulaney, C. *Methods for Teaching: A Skills Approach.* 2d. ed. Columbus, Ohio: Charles E. Merrill Publishing Co., 1985.

58. Jeter, J., and Davis, O. "Elementary School Teachers' Differential Classroom Interaction with Children as a Function of Differential Expectations of Pupil Achievements." Paper presented at the annual meeting of the American Educational Research Association, 1973.

59. Johnson, D. W., and Johnson, R. T. *Cooperation in the Classroom.* New Brighton, Minn: Interaction Book Co., 1984.

60. Johnson, D. W., and Johnson, R. T. *Learning Together and Alone: Cooperative, Competitive, and Individualistic Learning.* Englewood Cliffs, N.J.: Prentice-Hall, 1987.

61. Joyce, B., and Showers, B. "The Coaching of Teaching." *Educational Leadership* 40 (1982): 4–10.

62. Joyce, B., and Weil, M. *Models of Teaching.* 2d. ed. New York: Prentice-Hall, 1986.

63. Joyce, B.; Showers, B.; and Rolheiser-Bennett, C. "Staff Development and Student Learning: A Synthesis of Research on Models of Teaching." *Educational Leadership* 45 (1987): 11–23.

64. Kennedy, J. J.; Bush, A. J.; Cruickshank, D. K.; and Haefele, D. "Additional Investigations into the Nature of Teacher Clarity." Paper presented at the annual meeting of the American Educational Research Association, Toronto, March 1978.

65. Kierstead, J. "Direct Instruction and Experiential Approaches: Are They Really Mutually Exclusive?" *Educational Leadership* 42 (May 1985): 25–30

66. Lapp, D., et al. *Teaching and Learning: Philosophical, Psychological, Curricular Applications.* New York: Macmillan, 1975.

67. Livingston, S. A., and Stoll, C. S. *Simulation Games.* New York: Free Press, 1973.

68. Lovell, J. T., and Wiles, K. *Supervision for Better Schools.* 5th ed. Englewood Cliffs, N.J.: Prentice-Hall, 1983.

69. Manatt, R. P. *Evaluating Teacher Performance.* Videotape. Washington, D.C.: Association for Supervision and Curriculum Development, 1981.

70. Massialas, B. G., and Cox, C. B. *Inquiry in Social Studies.* New York: McGraw-Hill, 1966.

71. McDonald, F. J. "Research on Teaching: A Report on Phase II of the Beginning Teacher Evaluation Study." In *The Appraisal of Teaching Concepts and Processes*, edited by Gary D. Borich and Kathleen S. Fenton. Reading, Mass.: Addison-Wesley, 1977.

72. McFaul, S. A. "An Examination of Direct Instruction." *Educational Leadership* (April 1983): 67–69.

73. Medley, D. *Teacher Competency Testing and the Teacher Educator.* Charlottesville, Va.: Educational Research, School of Education, University of Virginia, 1982.

74. National Academy of Sciences. *Science and Creationism: A View from the National Academy of Sciences.* Washington, D.C.: National Academy Press, 1984.

75. Ornstein, A. C. "Research on Teaching: Issues and Trends." *Journal of Teacher Education* 36 (November/December 1985): 27–31.

76. Raths, J. "Enhancing Understanding Through Debriefing." *Educational Leadership* 54 (1987): 24–27.

77. Rebhorn, M. "Ideas for the Class." Quoted in article by C. Hosley. *Chronicle of Higher Education*, July 1, 1987, p. 11.

78. Reid, E. R. *Reader Newsletter.* Salt Lake City, Utah: Exemplary Center for Reading Instruction, 1980.

79. Reinhartz, D. "Myths of Classroom Teaching: A Humanistic Defense of the Lecture Method." Paper presented at a conference on the Teaching of History, North Texas State University, Denton, Texas, October 23–24, 1979.

80. _____. "Teaching History with Maps: A Graphic Dimension." In *Essays on Walter Prescott Webb and the Teaching of History,* edited by D. Reinhartz and S. E. Maizlish, pp. 79–98. College Station, Tex: Texas A&M University Press, 1985.

81. Reinhartz, J. "Middle School Instructional Strategies for Teaching Excellence." *Journal for Tennessee Middle School Association* 8 (Winter 1984): 25–35.

82. Reinhartz, J., and Beach, D. M. *Improving Middle School Instruction: A Research-Based Self-Assessment System.* Washington, D.C.: National Education Association, 1983.

83. Reinhartz, J., and Reinhartz, D. "Sensitizing Future Elementary Teachers to Sociocultural Diversity in the Classroom." In *Proceedings of the Eighth International Conference on Improving University Teaching,* West Berlin, Germany, 1982.

84. Reinhartz, J., and Van Cleaf, D. *Teach-Practice-Apply: The TPA Instruction Model, K–8.* Washington, D.C.: National Education Association, 1986.

85. Reynolds, J. "In Search of Mr./Ms. Goodteacher." *Action in Teacher Education* 11 (Winter 1979–1980): 35–38.

86. Rist, R. "Student Social Class and Teacher Expectations: The Self-Fulfilling Prophecy in Ghetto Education." *Harvard Educational Review* 40 (1970): 411–51.

87. Roemer, K. M. *Build Your Own Utopia: An Interdisciplinary Course in Utopian Speculation.* Washington, D.C.: University Press of America, 1981.

88. _____. "Using Utopia to Teach the 80's: A Case for Guided Design." *World Future Society Bulletin* (July-August 1985): 1–5.

89. Rogers, S. "If I Can See Myself, I Can Change." *Educational Leadership* 45 (October 1987): 64–67.

90. Rosenshine, B. "Content, Time, and Direct Instruction." In *Research on Teaching: Concepts, Findings, and Implications*, edited by P. L. Peterson and H. J. Walberg. Berkeley, Calif.: McCutchan Publishing Co., 1979.

91. _____. "Teaching Functions in Instructional Programs." *Elementary School Journal* 83 (1983): 335–52.

92. Rosenshine, B., and Furst, N. "Research in Teacher Performance Criteria." In *Research in Teacher Education*, edited by B. O. Smith. Englewood Cliffs, N.J.: Prentice-Hall, 1971.

93. Rowe, M. "Pausing Phenomena: Influence on the Quality of Instruction." *Journal of Psycholinguistic Research* 3 (1974): 203–24.

94. _____. "Wait-Time and Rewards as Instructional Variables— Their Influence on Language, Logic, and Fate Control: Part I— Wait Time." *Journal of Research in Science Teaching* 11 (1974): 81–94.

95. Rubin, L. *Artistry in Teaching.* New York: Random House, 1985.

96. Sergiovani, T., and Starratt, R. J. *Supervision: Human Perspectives.* 3d ed. New York: McGraw-Hill, 1983.

97. Sharan, S. "Cooperative Learning in Small Groups." *Review of Educational Research* 50 (1980): 241–71.

98. Sharan, S., and Sharan, Y. *Small-Group Teaching.* Englewood Cliffs, N.J.: Educational Technology Publications, 1976.

99. Showers, B. "Teachers Coaching Teachers." *Educational Leadership* 42 (1985): 43–48.

100. Sizer, T. R. "This Trivial, Bottom-Aching Thing We Call High School." *New York Times,* October 31, 1987.

101. Slavin, R. E. "Student Teams and Comparison Among Equals: Effects on Academic Performance and Student Attitudes." *Journal of Educational Psychology* 70 (1978): 532–38.

102. _____. "Cooperative Learning." *Review of Educational Research* 50 (1980): 317–43.

103. _____. "Effects of Student Teams and Peer Tutoring on Academic Achievement and Time on Task." *Journal of Experimental Education* 48 (1980): 252–57.

104. _____. "Synthesis of Research on Cooperative Learning." *Educational Leadership* (May 1981): 655–60.

105. _____. "A Case Study of Psychological Research Affecting Classroom Practice: Student Team Learning." *Elementary School Journal* 82 (September 1981): 5–17.

106. _____. *Student Team Learning: An Overview and Practical Guide.* 2d ed. Washington, D.C.: National Education Association, 1988.

107. _____. "Learning Together." *American Education* 10 (Summer 1986): 6–11.

108. _____. *Cooperative Learning: Student Teams.* 2d ed. Washington, D.C.: National Education Association, 1987.

109. Slavin, R. E.; Leavey, M.; and Madden, N. *Student Teams and Individualized Instruction: Effects on Student Achievement, Attitudes, and Behaviors.* Baltimore: Center for Social Organization of Schools, Johns Hopkins University, 1981.

110. Smith, R. A. "A Teacher's Views on Cooperative Learning." *Phi Delta Kappan* 68 (May 1987): 663–66.

111. Stallings, J. A., and Kaskowitz, D. *Follow Through Classroom Observation Evaluation, 1972–1973.* Menlo Park, Calif.: Stanford Research Institute, 1974.

112. Stallings, J. A.; Needels, M.; and Stayrook, N. *How to Change the Process of Teaching Basic Reading Skills in Secondary Schools.* Menlo Park, Calif.: SRI International, 1979.

113. Stone, C. "A Meta-Analysis of Advance Organizer Studies." *Journal of Experimental Education* 51 (1983): 194–99.

114. Sunal, C. S., and Hatcher, B. A. "Studying History Through Art." *Social Education*, How to Do It Series 5, 50 (April/May 1986): 1–8.

115. Swann, W., and Snyder, M. "On Translating Beliefs into Action: Theories of Ability and Their Application in an Instructional Setting." *Journal of Personality and Social Psychology* 38 (1980): 879–88.

116. Taba, H. *Teaching Strategies and Cognitive Functioning in Elementary School Children.* Cooperative Research Project 2404.

San Francisco: San Francisco State College, 1966.

117. Taebel, D. A. "Educational Games and the Political Process." *Southwestern Journal of Social Education* 3 (Spring-Summer 1973): 18-20.

118. _____. *The Precinct Convention Game (PRECON)*. Arlington, Tex.: Institute of Urban Studies, University of Texas at Arlington, 1972.

119. Taylor, D. "Second Grade Reading Instruction: The Teacher-Child Dyadic Interaction of Boys and Girls of Varying Abilities." Master's thesis, Rutgers University, 1977.

120. Taylor J., and Walford, R. *Simulation in the Classroom*. Baltimore, Md.: Penguin Education, 1974.

121. Walberg, H. J.; Schiller, D.; and Haertel, G. D. "The Quiet Revolution in Educational Research." *Phi Delta Kappan* (November 1979): 179–83.

122. Warner, A. R. "Alternative Certification and Ethical Responsibilities." *Social Education* (April/May 1986): 237.

123. Weinstein, R. "Reading Group Membership in First Grade: Teacher Behaviors and Pupil Experience over Time." *Journal of Educational Psychology* 68 (1976): 103–16.

124. Wildman, T. M., and Niles, J. A. "Essentials of Professional Growth." *Educational Leadership* 44 (February 1987): 4–10.